Fascinating Stories for Curious Minds

Unbelievable True Tales Across Science, History, Space, Pop Culture, the Natural World and Beyond

Bobbie Oakey

Thank you for buying our book!

If you find this storybook fun and useful, we would be very grateful if you could post a short review on Amazon! Your support does make a difference and we read every review personally.

If you would like to leave a review, just head on over to this book's Amazon page and click "Write a customer review."

Thank you for your support!

Contents

Introduction

Welcome to *Fascinating Stories for Curious Minds*! In the pages that follow, you'll embark on a journey through the most astonishing corners of our reality. From the peculiar prestige of pineapples to the remarkable resilience of tardigrades, each story is a gateway into the wonders and oddities of our world and beyond.

This collection of true stories will take you from the glowing creatures in the ocean's depths to the ancient to long-lived trees that dot the landscape of our planet. You'll hear about inventors whose names got lost in history, and the small but mighty organisms that keep our world in balance.

Get ready to explore the extremes of the Earth, the quirks of the animal kingdom, the peculiarities of science and much more. Brace yourself for a journey into knowledge—it's going to be both enlightening and entertaining!

When Owning a Pineapple Was a Status Symbol

You can typically spot a wealthy person by the car they drive, how much jewelry they wear, or by their expensive clothing. But, only a couple hundred years ago, you could spot a wealthy person by a pineapple.

These days, the pineapple is a common fruit, readily available in any grocery store. But, back then, they were a rarity and were highly prized. They were first discovered by Columbus on his voyage to the Americas in 1492, and he named them "Pina" because of their resemblance to a pinecone. The first account of them in Europe was in the 1600s. There was no cold storage for shipping items in those days. With the long sea voyage across the Atlantic, many of the fruit deteriorated. So, they were only available in small quantities to those rich enough to afford them. Being seen with a pineapple was an immediate indication of wealth – in the 1700s, it is estimated that the cost of a single pineapple in today's money would be around $8,000.

Pineapple owners were actually reluctant to eat them because it would mean giving up this status symbol. Instead, they were used as a centerpiece on the banquet table or as a work of art on a shelf. It was only when they started to go rotten that they would actually be eaten. Poorer people who wanted to make their friends jealous of their extravagance could rent one for the night when they were having a dinner party from one of the many "pineapple rental" shops.

It was also quite common for wealthy people to carry a pineapple around with them as a display of their riches, like someone who might wear an expensive watch or a gold chain. They were so sought after those people who could not afford to buy or rent one could buy dishes and teapots in the shape of a pineapple.

Of course, there were some who tried to take advantage of their great value. In the early 1800s, there were a number of court cases involving pineapple theft, and in one notorious case, a man was sentenced in the Old Bailey to seven years of hard labor in Australia for stealing seven pineapples.

The pineapple later came to symbolize generosity and hospitality. Napkins and tablecloths were decorated with drawings of pineapple to make guests feel welcome. Bedposts in guest bedrooms were carved with pineapple shapes. The gateposts at the entrance to many large houses had stone pineapples on top as a sign of welcome, and some of these can still be seen today.

Later, in the Victorian era, steamships were able to cross the ocean more quickly, and pineapples started to be imported in abundance. They were now available to everyone, so the symbol of wealth was lost.

So, next time you buy a pineapple, remember that a few hundred years ago, you would've needed to be very rich to enjoy what you can now.

Animals That Glow in the Dark

Scientists in China have managed to make pigs glow in the dark. They recently announced that they have developed at least 10 piglets that can glow green in the dark when seen under ultra-violet light. They did this by injecting substances from jellyfish into the baby pig's cells while they were still inside the mother pig. Jellyfish are well known for glowing in the deepest parts of the ocean, where the Sun never reaches, and they have now helped create glowing pigs.

Of course, you might think this is very interesting, but why would they spend all this time and research just to make pigs that glow? Well, this wasn't just done for fun. This helped develop techniques that will hopefully make better medicines in the future.

Researchers hope this will show them how to create "enzymes," which can help with diseases and illnesses. Doing this with animals is better and cheaper than building huge laboratories and research centers.

Even though the piglets have been "genetically engineered," they can still lead normal lives. In fact, the piglets don't notice a difference. This is also not the only time glowing animals have been created.

Using the same technique, scientists in Turkey have made glowing rabbits. They believe this will allow them to produce medicines in the bodies of rabbits. They can then get that medicine from the female rabbits' milk without causing harm to the animals.

The same procedures have been used to save endangered animals such as American Wildcats. Researchers are also developing clones of the wildcats by injecting them with the cells from glowing jellyfish so they can easily identify them. So, if you are outside at night and you see some green glowing animals, don't worry, it's just a science experiment.

The World's Slowest Marathon Runner

One of the main events of the Summer Olympics, and one of the most popular, is the marathon, which is usually won by a competitor running the 26-mile course in less than three hours. Most runners will complete it in less than four hours. But would you believe one runner took more than 50 years to complete the marathon?

Japanese athlete Shizo Kanakuri was a world record holder who had finished a marathon in Japan in what was, then, a record time of 2 hours and 32 minutes. He was also considered to be the favorite to win the marathon at the 1912 Olympics in Stockholm, the capital of Sweden.

Although Kanakuri was a fast runner, he was young and inexperienced at the age of 20. His first hurdle was getting to Stockholm in time for the event.

He had to take an 18-day journey from Japan to Sweden by ship and train. He kept fit by running around the ship and train stations whenever they were stopped. When he finally arrived in the capital, there was no food like what he was used to, so he had to eat European food. This ended up giving him stomach issues.

Then, his training was interrupted by his coach being hospitalized for the whole tournament. Kanakuri's teammates also fell ill, so he was alone in a strange country.

The day of the race arrived, and it was an unusually hot day. Many runners even dropped out of the race due to the heatwave. On that day, 68 runners had entered, but only half of them crossed the finish line.

After about 16 miles, Kanakuri collapsed with heat exhaustion and was cared for by a local farmer and his family. Kanakuri, embarrassed by his failure to finish the race, quietly went home as soon as he recovered, but unlike the other runners who dropped out, he did not notify the Olympic officials. So, they simply recorded him as "missing."

Back home in Japan, he continued running marathons and even returned to Europe to compete in Belgium and France. After more than 50 years, in 1967, Kanakuri was contacted by a Swedish TV station who heard the story of "the missing runner." They made him an offer to return to Sweden to complete the race that he started years before.

Kanakuri agreed, and at the age of 75, he finally finished the Swedish Olympic marathon. He had once held the world record for the fastest marathon. He also holds the record for the world's slowest marathon: 54 years, eight months, six days, five hours, and 32 minutes.

When the Universe was Small Enough to be Held in Your Hand

Most people have heard of the Big Bang Theory, which is a theory on how the universe started. It is actually a strange story, but scientists and physicists have studied the origin of the universe for decades, and this is the most likely explanation.

In the beginning, there was nothing. Then suddenly, a small dot appeared, which scientists call a "singularity." This small point was less than a billionth of a millimeter, the smallest thing that has ever existed. Where it came from – that is something that no scientist has ever begun to speculate; it is completely unknown.

Within milliseconds, the singularity exploded. At first, it was the size of a golf ball. If we had been around in those days, we would have been able to hold the entire universe in one hand. Then, within a period of time so short it could not be recorded on any equipment – estimated as a hundredth of a billionth of a trillionth of a millisecond – the universe expanded again at the speed of light and is still expanding. Given the current rate of expansion, scientists can work backward and estimate the age of the universe at 13.8 billion years.

As the universe expanded, it started to cool down and form sub-atomic particles, which became atoms in the shape of clouds of gas, such as hydrogen and helium. As these cooled, they formed stars and galaxies, and their gravitational fields pulled in clouds of dust that eventually formed together and made planets.

There are still things about the universe that no scientist understands, for example, "dark matter." This is similar to the state of everything before the origin of the universe. It seems that, in space, there are huge areas, billions of light years wide, where there is nothing, not even space, just an empty darkness. Telescopes cannot see through it, and no one knows what it is, except that it is there.

Something surprising but obvious when you think about it is that the universe does not go on forever. It has an endpoint, but we can never find it because it is continuously expanding, with the endpoint getting further and further away. No matter how fast we traveled through space, we would never reach the end. This puts a lot into perspective.

Humans have been on the planet for around 200,000 years, which was estimated by the oldest human remains ever found. In comparison to all life in the universe, it is like filling a bath to the brim with water and adding one more tiny water droplet. Humans are that droplet.

The 18th Century Chess Robot

It is generally believed that machines with artificial intelligence (AI) that can play chess and even defeat human chess champions are a recent invention. In fact, we believe the first chess-playing computer was created in 1957, although it took up to 8 minutes to work out each move – it has been calculated that there are more possible moves on a chess board than there are stars that can be seen in the night sky, so it was a difficult task for an early computer.

The first AI machine to play chess was actually invented around 1770 in Austria by Wolfgang Von Kempelen to impress Queen Marie-Theresa. It was a big wooden box with a tabletop designed like a chess board. A wooden figure sat at the table dressed in a robe and turban, with an exotic Eastern look, and was called "the Turk."

Kempelen claimed the Turk could beat anyone at chess. So, the best players from across the land were summoned to the royal court to play against the machine. When a player was seated opposite the Turk, Kempelen turned a crank at the side of the box, and the dummy came to life. It would turn its head side to side, reach out to grasp a pawn with its hand and play a game of chess.

The Turk beat every player, and it became a sensation in the royal court. In 1783, Kempelen took the Turk on a tour of Europe across England, Germany, and France, beating every player who challenged it. In Paris, it even beat the great Benjamin Franklin, who, at that time, was serving as the US Ambassador to France.

Kempelen died in 1804, and the Turk was bought by a German showman, Johann Maelzel, who toured the world with it. Maelzel also installed a voice box that could say "Check" and "Checkmate" at the appropriate times. In Vienna in 1809, the Turk played against Napoleon Bonaparte, who tried to cheat with illegal chess moves, but each time, the Turk shook its head, moved the chess piece back to its original position, and won the game.

Over the years, many people tried to understand how it worked, and many were convinced it was a fraud, but the Turk kept its secrets until 1838 when Maelzel died on a ship while taking the Turk to Philadelphia. The machine was sold to a group led by a doctor, John Mitchell, who wanted to unravel the secret of the machine.

When they took it apart, they found that it was indeed a fraud. There was a small space inside the table box where a man could sit and direct the dummy by controlling levers and buttons moving the head, arms, and hands. The difficult part of keeping the fraud up was finding a man small enough to fit inside who was also a chess expert. One advantage this person had was that anyone playing against the Turk would be distracted by the strange machine and would not concentrate on the game as much as they usually would – a good advantage in a game where high concentration is essential.

The Turk was donated to a museum in Philadelphia, where it lay forgotten for many years until one night in July of 1854 when the museum caught fire. Doctor Mitchell's son, Silas, rushed to the museum to try to save it from the flames, but it was too late. Silas later wrote an article explaining all the secrets and travels of this strange chess-playing machine, and he concluded the article by swearing he heard the machine say a final "Checkmate" as it burned.

What's the Largest Organ in the Human Body?

You might know that an adult human skeleton has 206 bones. You might even know that, amazingly, there are more bones in our hands and feet together than in any other part of our body. But have you ever thought about the different sizes of organs in the human body and which one is the largest?

Opinions vary, but many scientists and doctors agree that the largest organ in the human body is the one that we can all see every day – the skin. If we could remove all our skin at once, it would weigh around 8 pounds. It would cover around 2 square meters. This is for an average adult human.

Our skin acts like a shield. It's waterproof and keeps us safe from extreme temperatures. It protects us from sunlight and helps us filter chemicals. It helps keep viruses out and also allows us to excrete waste and harmful substances through our sweat. Healthy skin is smooth, with no cuts or breaks.

Our skin also helps us sense what's around us so we can relate to the outside world. If we touch something prickly, like a needle, we know to pull our hand away quickly. When exposed to sunlight, our skin manufactures Vitamin D. This "sunshine vitamin" is required to convert calcium into healthy, strong bones.

There are three layers to the skin. The outer layer, the epidermis, is formed from dead skin cells overlapping in layers. These layers are constantly replaced with living cells from the layers below. The middle layer, the dermis, gives our skin its elasticity and strength and helps regulate our body temperature. Finally, the subcutis has a seam of fat, which is laid down to act as a fuel reserve in case food is in short supply. The subcutis also helps by acting as a cushion against falls.

The skin is our largest external organ, but there are organs inside our bodies that are larger. This is where some doctors and scientists have their own opinions about what's really the largest organ in the body. Some argue that the skeleton is the largest organ. The skin accounts for around 5.5% to 8% of a typical human's body weight, but the skeleton accounts for around 14%.

And the largest solid internal organ? That's the liver, which typically weighs around 3 to 3.5 pounds. Your liver helps process poisons and other harmful substances known as toxins; it stores nutrients and vitamins, produces blood, and helps you fight off infections.

As for the most important organ in the body, the brain typically weighs a little less in adults than the liver – around 3 pounds. A newborn baby's brain is very small, weighing a little more than three-quarters of a pound.

Tardigrades: The Toughest Creature on Earth?

What animal springs to mind when you think about the toughest creatures on this amazing planet of ours? Maybe you think of lions, tigers, bears, or sharks. But, you probably wouldn't think about tardigrades – even though these tiny creatures are truly astonishing.

They look like something out of a science fiction movie, with plump bodies and a kind of sucker-shaped opening where you'd expect the mouth to be. Most tardigrades only eat plant materials, but some are carnivores and eat animal flesh. The spear-like structures near the mouth are used to pierce individual plant cells and suck out the contents. (The scientific name for this is *buccopharyngeal apparatus*.)

They have short bodies with four fused segments. Every segment has a pair of short and stout limbs with no joints, and at the end of each limb, you'll find sets of four to six sharp claws. The head region of a tardigrade is very well-developed.

Tardigrades are considered to be aquatic creatures since their bodies need to be surrounded by a thin layer of water. They're thought to be closely related to insects and crustaceans, and they are tiny – usually only about one millimeter long.

They might look soft and a little bit squishy from the outside, but tardigrades dwell inside a tough outer coating called a cuticle, not unlike a praying mantis or grasshopper. We've known about them since at least 1773 when a German scientist named Johann August Ephraim Goeze described them as "little water bears" due to the way they moved. A few years later, an Italian priest and biologist called

Lazzaro Spallanzani came up with the name "tardigrade," which roughly means "slow stepper."

When they dry out, tardigrades are around 33% of their normal size. They stop breathing, moving, or doing much else. This is what scientists call their "tun" state. And they can stay like this for years – until they come across water once again.

Scientists think it's a molecule called trehalose that allows them to go into this state – it preserves the outer cell membranes. The cells are much less likely to rupture if they dry out or if ice crystals form inside the tardigrade's body.

What makes tardigrades so amazing is that they can live just about anywhere: in the sea, freshwater, moss, flowering plants, sand. They can live in places where the temperature is just above absolute zero, the temperature at which all molecular motion ceases, and can survive temperatures higher than the boiling point of water. They can live in places where the pressure is six times greater than at the deepest point of the ocean. And they can live up to 30 years without food or water.

If it's a damp day, and you can borrow a microscope and find a damp environment like moss, you might be able to see tardigrades. They look something like a very small cross between a caterpillar and a woodlouse. Oh, and there are around 1,300 species known so far.

What do Astronauts Eat in Space

If you've ever visited a science museum with space travel exhibits, you might have seen freeze-dried ice cream. All the water has been removed to make it light and portable – ideal for taking on a spacecraft, you might think. It isn't quite that simple, however.

On Earth, growing or manufacturing our own food can be relatively straightforward. While different crops grow better in different soils and climates, typically, when we plant crops, they grow toward the light. We harvest them, eat them, and the cycle starts again.

In space, however, things are different, with a lack of gravity being one of the major issues. Even on a spacecraft, there is only what is known as microgravity. How does a fruit or a vegetable even know which way to grow if it can't tell which way is up or down?

So, what do astronauts eat?

The Soviet Union's Yuri Gagarin was the first man in space in 1961. For his first meal, he had chocolate sauce and pureed meat squeezed out of tubes like toothpaste. A year later, John Glenn was the first American to eat a meal in space. It quickly became all too apparent that rehydrating freeze-dried food wasn't as easy as it might have seemed. A nozzle had to be used to inject the water, and the package was then kneaded (like bread) so the food could be reconstituted. It was then squeezed straight into the mouth – not exactly fine dining!

On later American missions, astronauts ate various foods. As part of the Apollo 8 mission in 1968, the astronauts ate turkey with cranberry sauce and dressing. And by the time of Apollo 11, when Neil

Armstrong and his crew landed on the moon for the first time, the meals were a little more sophisticated.

The Apollo 11 astronauts were the first men in space who had hot water and were able to eat with a spoon from their food packages. While on board, both Buzz Aldrin and Neil Armstrong ate beef and vegetables, Canadian bacon and apple sauce, and pork with potato scallops.

"Meal A," the first meal consumed by humans on the moon, included canned peaches. There were also sugar cookie cubes, bacon squares, a drink made with grapefruit and pineapple juice, and coffee. For their second meal on the moon, they had beef stew, chicken soup, an orange-based drink, grape punch, and a fruitcake.

More recently, astronauts have managed to grow food in space. In 1982, a plant called Arabidopsis was grown on the Soviet Salyut 7, and in 2015, American astronauts ate "space lettuce" for the first time. In 2020, meanwhile, NASA astronaut Kate Rubins harvested the first-ever crop of radishes on the International Space Station.

You might be surprised to find out that bread isn't allowed in space. Anything with crumbs is just too difficult to eat and risks major damage to the expensive and specialist machinery on board.

One final curious fact – "space ice cream" didn't actually make its way into outer space. NASA decided it was just too crumbly!

The Amazing Tomato: Fruit, Vegetable, or Something In-Between?

It's easy to tell the difference between fruits and vegetables, right?

The term "fruit" is usually used to describe fleshy, sweet botanical fruits high in fructose, a natural sugar. "Vegetables" are typically a little sour or savory in flavor and not so high in fructose. Like so many things in life, however, it's not quite that simple.

Think for a minute about all those lovely fruits that you see blossoming in the spring – apples, apricots, mangos, melons, peaches, and pears. They start as flowers, they're fertilized with pollen (often by bees or other insects), and then they slowly turn into seeds that we can eat.

Vegetables, on the other hand, are any edible part of a plant that isn't a fruit. That might be flowers, leaves, roots, stems, and tubers. It could be beets, cabbage, carrots, lettuce, spinach, stems, spinach, potatoes, onions, broccoli, and cauliflower. Tomatoes and potatoes are actually distant cousins, but since potatoes aren't "fruit of the vine" but rather root vegetables, they don't fit the definition of a fruit.

So, by that definition, bean pods, cucumbers, corn kernels, eggplants, pumpkins, squash, and tomatoes are also fruits.

You might think that tomatoes are, obviously, a fruit. They start as flowers, produce edible pods and seeds, and when they're mature, we eat them in all kinds of dishes, from pizza to salad.

Actually, the tomato plant itself is a seed plant that grows red tomatoes that are edible and used in many dishes, from pizza to casseroles to salads.

The final fate of the humble tomato in the United States was decided toward the end of the nineteenth century. A merchant named John Nix had been going about his business, importing some West Indian tomatoes through the Port of New York.

The customs official on duty, a man by the name of Edward Hedden, quoted a piece of law called the Tariff Act of 1883. He demanded that a 10% tax should be paid as "foreign vegetables" attracted an import duty.

Nix pointed out the tomato was not a vegetable; it was a fruit. And he shouldn't have to pay any tax. Sadly, Nix lost. In 1893, a judge called Horace Gray ruled that a tomato was a vegetable, mainly because people mainly ate it with meat, fish, or soup and not as a dessert.

All kinds of similar rulings followed at the Supreme Court, although things were a little different in Europe, where the European Union declared in 2001 that carrots, sweet potatoes, and tomatoes were actually fruits.

Not all states agreed, though. Ohio and Tennessee decided that the tomato was going to be their state fruit, while Arkansas decided the tomato was both a fruit and a vegetable. While Louisiana declared that the tomato was the official "vegetable plant" of the state.

So, is a tomato a fruit? Or is a tomato a vegetable? Well, in fact, it's both – depending on your point of view.

Is There Water on Mars?

Our nearest neighbors in the solar system are the Moon, Venus, and Mars, and all of them have fascinated scientists for centuries. Water covers around three-quarters of the Earth's surface, but what about other planets?

For a long time, it was thought that there was water on the moon, and the same was true of Mars. In Victorian times, many astronomers were interested in Mars, including an Italian called Giovanni Virginio Schiaparelli. He called the dark areas on Mars seas, while the light areas were continents. He also saw what came to be called Canali on Mars - and although the word means channel, many people at the time thought this meant canals. The Suez Canal was completed in 1969, and Mars caught the imagination.

Another astronomer, American Percival Lowel, decided in 1894 that the canals were real, and this gave rise to the belief that intelligent life had created the canals on the Red Planet. Astronomers of the time thought their purpose had been to carry water to areas at the equator on Mars from the polar caps.

In England, a young writer named H.G. Wells was full of enthusiasm for the idea of life on Mars. In 1898, he published one of his most famous novels, The War of the Worlds, and the planet was very popular with many writers over the next few decades.

It wasn't until Mariner 4 flew close to Mars in 1965 that we found out the canals weren't real; however, humans love to find patterns in the world to help make sense of it. That doesn't mean there's no water on Mars, however. Some recent space missions have been on the hunt for water near the surface of Mars. And at the end of 2021, water was found on Mars - in the region we currently call the Grand Canyon.

The snappily named ESA-Roscosmos ExoMars Trace Gas Orbiter (TGO for short) has now found water below the surface of Mars. It has an instrument known as FREND (Fine Resolution Epithermal Neutron Detector), which is creating a map of hydrogen on Martian soil: the presence of hydrogen can be used to measure the water content.

What makes this so exciting is that until now, we've thought most of the water on Mars is at the poles, in the form of ice. TGO makes it possible to look for water up to one meter below the dust that covers most of the surface of Mars.

FREND takes a different approach to hunting for water - it isn't looking for light but for neutrons. There are more neutrons in drier soils than in wetter ones - and scientists can now see things they haven't previously seen. FREND may be detecting water that is still in the form of ice, but even if that is the case, it's an incredibly exciting development, particularly as most of the future missions to Mars will probably land at lower latitudes.

Why Clouds Are White

There are so many fascinating questions to consider when it comes to nature – like why are clouds white?

Well, first of all, not all clouds are white. Two different factors determine whether our eyes perceive clouds as grey or white. In fact, at certain times of day, we might see clouds as more of a pink or peach shade.

Why is this?

You probably already know that light comes to us from the Sun. We see sunlight as white, although visible light is made up of several colors. We see the entire spectrum when a ray of light hits a prism or a water droplet, and it splits into the seven colors of the rainbow: red, orange, yellow, green, blue, indigo, and violet.

The water droplets inside the clouds are much larger than the particles in our atmosphere that exist in the sky. When the Sun's light heads toward the surface of the Earth and hits a cloud, it interacts with the water droplets inside that cloud.

The solid water and liquid particles inside a cloud are called hydrometeors – and they're what give clouds their color. When the concentration and size of those hydrometeors are higher, it's more and more difficult for sunlight to make its way into the cloud. Those heavy, large hydrometeors are the ones that cause rain or snow, as they fall more easily from the clouds.

When the cloud is made up mainly of ice crystals and small droplets, the sunlight that can get inside the cloud gets scattered over several points. These are the kinds of clouds that we see as bright white. When the light gets scattered inside a cloud, it is usually sent upward again. Sometimes, it gets sent to the sides of the cloud.

If you've ever looked at clouds, you might have noticed that the sides and top of the cloud are whiter than the base – this is because the base does not receive as much light.

Clouds can look red or orange at sunset or sunrise, and this is because the Sun is low in the sky at these times of the day. Light from the Sun has to work much harder to travel through the atmosphere, and as a result, a higher proportion of blue light is deflected away as it is scattered; more yellow and red light reaches the Earth. What we see is a sort of pink or peachy glow.

Every visible color has a wavelength of its own, from short to long. We could get really technical about this, but nanometers are the units used to measure the wavelengths of light. At the 700 nanometers spot, red light is the "longest" light we can see; blue is the "shortest" at 400 nanometers.

So, there you have it – clouds appear white if more light is reaching them from the Sun. The amount of light, and therefore the color of the cloud, can be affected by those crazy little hydrometeors.

The Truth About the Mary Celeste

Most people have heard the strange tale of the ship the Mary Celeste, sometimes called the Marie Celeste. A merchant ship, a brigantine with two masts, the Mary Celeste, was spotted drifting near the Azores – a group of islands in the Atlantic Ocean about 1,200 miles off the coast of Portugal – by the British ship the Dei Gratia, whose captain, David Morehouse, recognized the ship as one that had set sail from New York eight days before, bound for Genoa in Italy.

Captain Morehouse sent a boarding party over to the Mary Celeste to offer help. The boarding party found no one aboard. All the crew's belongings were still in their quarters, there was a six-month supply of food and water, and the cargo of industrial alcohol in 1,700 wooden barrels seemed intact, but there was no sign of the crewmen and no indication of what happened. However, the ship's lifeboat was missing, all the cargo hatches were propped open, and a long rope was trailing behind the ship. So started one of the most mystifying and enduring puzzles in the history of the oceans. What had happened to the ten crew members – had they abandoned the ship in the lifeboat? But why? The ship seemed completely seaworthy; there was no indication of a struggle that might have been signs of a mutiny, an attack by pirates, or just violent disagreements between the crew.

Theories have included scenarios like an attack by a killer octopus or other sea monsters or a giant waterspout. Or an event that scared the crew so much they decided to leave the ship and escape in the lifeboat. Actually, according to the latest theories, this is close to what happened, and the long trailing rope behind the ship was a vital clue.

Also, nine of the 1,700 barrels in the hold were empty. At first, there were theories that the contents had been drunk by the crew, but this was industrial ethyl alcohol, and even one cup would make someone violently ill. So, it was highly unlikely that all nine barrels had been consumed.

Then, it became apparent that nearly all the barrels in the hold were made from white oak, with the exception of the nine empty ones, which were made from red oak. Red oak is porous and must have been used by mistake. The theory is that, over the course of the voyage, the red oak barrels leaked alcohol fumes, which built up to the point where the crew was starting to become sick, so they opened all the hatches, lowered the lifeboat, and all got off the ship to wait in clearer air until the fumes had dissipated.

To stop from drifting off, they tied a rope from the stern of the ship to the lifeboat. Of course, they left all their possessions and supplies onboard, thinking they would be back within a day or so. A storm blew up, and the rope broke, and the lifeboat lost touch with the ship. The crew probably started to row, but it seems they were lost in the rough seas. The ship continued to drift until it was eventually spotted.

While no one will ever know what really happened, this is the most likely explanation. However, the story of Mary Celeste was, and maybe still is, one of the greatest mysteries of the seas.

Do We Just Use 10% of Our Brains?

This is something we often hear that most of us only use 10% of our brains. Some people have made their fortune by selling systems and books teaching people how to use more of their brain so that they will be smarter and more successful, and regularly, we see ads for things that promise to "increase your brain power."

However, it is all a complete myth – our bodies are designed so that we use 100% of our brain every day, and the only situation where this is less is in the case of damage or disease in the brain, like a stroke, which impairs some functions.

It's almost laughable: imagine having something as wonderful and sophisticated as a human brain and letting 90% of it go to waste. But that is what many people believe, and others try to use this to make a living off gullible folk.

It is also not true that some creatures, such as dolphins, are smarter than humans. They seem smart because they have very simple lives on a single plane of existence – the sea – and what they do, they do very well. But what makes the human brain so superior is the many-layered cortical networks that control the flow and processing of information in the brain. The human cortex is large and complex, whereas most other mammals, including dolphins and whales, have simpler, smaller cortical networks. That is why a dolphin can never write anything like a work of Shakespeare and could never even read one.

There is no danger of any part of a healthy brain not being used. The danger comes from potential brain damage from stroke and things like dementia and Alzheimer's, which can limit the way a brain can be used.

There are many things we can do to protect the brain and keep it working, like regular exercise, a healthy diet, reduction in stress levels, and sleep. Sleep is the time when a brain doesn't have so much to do to keep us moving around, so it consolidates its storage, checks for errors, and reviews its memory system, a process we call dreaming. Sleep is one of the most important things we can do.

Brains have immense capacity. In your computer, tablet, or smartphone, you might have storage memory of anything from 50 to 500 gigabytes of storage, but in the brain, the neurons combine to help each other and to constantly regenerate, so the total memory capacity of a normal brain is around one million gigabytes. In theory, you have enough brain storage so that it can contain everything you have ever learned in your life. You may not recall it all, but it is all there, and if you don't always remember something, maybe you are not trying hard enough!

The Earth has Three Moons, Not Just One

Throughout all time, man has looked up in the night sky to see the stars and the moon. As familiar as our own face in a mirror, the moon has always been there, from a full moon to a slim crescent, and has been studied, photographed, even landed on, and is part of our lives. But what would you say if I told you we actually had three moons? I am sure the first question would be, "Where?"

A moon is defined as a celestial body that orbits a planet, and the two extra moons were first observed as recently as 1961. More studies have confirmed their existence, although some researchers insist on calling them pseudo-satellites. They are actually two giant clouds of dust, about 9 times bigger than our planet. The particles that form them are minute, the size of, well, dust particles. Despite their size, they are very hard to see, being almost transparent, but they are definitely there, orbiting Earth alongside our normal moon. Of course, being clouds of dust, it will not be possible to visit them; there is nothing to land on.

They are named after the astronomer who first identified them in the 1960s, Kazimierz Kordylewski, and known as Kordylewski clouds. They are difficult to detect because they are clouds, light from stars and the galaxy shines through them, and some astronomers call them "ghost moons." The dust clouds themselves are ancient and have been there since the dawn of time, although it has not always been the same dust in them. They are composed of particles that float through space and become stuck in Earth's orbit, gathering together and caught up in the cloud formations. The dust comes from other bodies throughout the solar system – planets, meteors, asteroids, and comets.

What is fascinating is not just that there are two moons that, up to 60 odd years ago, we knew nothing about, but they are composed of the detritus of the universe, a rare collection of particles from all over the galaxy like a museum of space we will never get to visit.

The Danish Navy Oaks

These days tree planting to regenerate forests and help the planet is considered an excellent way to care for the environment and is encouraged by all. However, one of the biggest tree plantings in history came about not from concern for the planet but as a consequence of a fierce naval battle.

In 1807, Britain and Denmark were at war. The reasons for this were complex and political at the time, involving alliances with France and Russia, and are no longer important except to historians who study that period. Nevertheless, they were at war, and Britain sent a fleet of warships under the command of its most famous sailor, Admiral Horatio Nelson, to attack the Danish fleet at Copenhagen.

One thing that battle is well known for is a quote from Admiral Nelson. At one point, a number of Danish ships were seen by another British ship to be getting ready to attack Nelson's flagship, and a signal was sent to Nelson advising him to retreat. Nelson, who had lost an eye in a previous sea battle, put his telescope to the patch over his blind eye and said, "I see no ships." He did not retreat and won the battle.

As a consequence, the Danish navy was destroyed. Those ships that were not sunk in the battle were captured by the British as prizes and taken back to England, where they were refitted, renamed, and sold as merchant ships. This left the Danish government in a difficult situation. There was no question that during this age of conflict, a well-equipped navy was necessary not only to wage war on enemies but also to protect the countries' ports and merchant shipping, and they had not one single ship left. This was the era of the wooden ship, and the most suitable timber for shipbuilding was the oak tree, of which Denmark was in short supply.

It was not possible to buy from other countries – they all faced the same issues, and even allies wanted their oak trees for their own ships. So, in 1810, a royal decree was issued to plant a new oak forest to provide the wood to rebuild the Danish navy, and 90,000 oak trees were planted.

What seems to have been overlooked was the fact that to be suitable for shipbuilding purposes, an oak tree takes around 200 years to grow to full maturity.

Over the succeeding 200 years, shipbuilding changed, and with technological developments, naval vessels started to be made from iron. So, the vast oak forests in Denmark became obsolete and unneeded. Still, the Association of Royal Foresters cared for the trees and kept an eye on them until, over time, this agency was replaced by The Danish Nature Agency, which took over management of the oak forest.

Finally, in 2007, nearly 200 years later, the Danish Nature Agency sent a message to the Danish Defense Minister: "Sir, your trees are ready."

Two of the trees were cut down to make replica Viking ships. The rest of the forest still stands as a reminder that we should always think carefully before making such big decisions.

The River that Runs Both Ways

The Tonle Sap River runs from the Tonle Sap Lake in the heart of Cambodia to the capital, Phnom Penh, which is 70 miles away. It irrigates the rice fields and other farm crops and sustains life in the countryside. Flowing through the capital city, it meets the mighty Mekong, which enters Cambodia from Laos, and they join forces on their way to the sea. Just about every river flows from its origin down to the sea, and that course never changes. But, this river is strangely unique in that once every year, it reverses its course and flows backward to the lake, the only river in the world to do so.

What actually happens is that the Mekong River, one of the world's largest, originates in the melting snow of the Tibetan Himalayan mountains, down into China, and then flows through Myanmar, Thailand, and Laos before reaching Cambodia. During the monsoon season, from about April to October, it is swollen with heavy rains in each of the countries it flows through, arriving in Phnom Penh with enough force to push the Tonle Sap all the way back to its starting point in the lake. This floods and irrigates the Cambodian rice fields and farmland, and its benefits are incalculable.

However, in the past two years, the changing climate patterns around the world have also affected the amount of rainfall from the monsoons, and the flows of the Mekong have been reduced. In addition, a number of new dams have been built along its course in China and Laos to generate hydroelectric power for those countries, which has also restricted water levels. This has weakened the reversal of the Tonle Sap, and water management experts are concerned that the days of the two-way river may be numbered.

So, it looks like man's efforts to develop the hydro potential of the Mekong River, combined with the effects of climate change on the monsoon, may spell the end of this Southeast Asian miracle – an ecological and economic disaster.

The Building That Melted Cars

London, England, is not particularly known for its hot weather, even in the summer months. However, in one area, at least, that is changing. On Fenchurch Street, in the central city, there has been a disturbing outbreak of extremely high temperatures, causing damage and destruction, and it is actually a man-made problem.

It is all because of the construction of a new skyscraper known as the Walkie-Talkie. This 525-foot tall building is shaped like a Walkie Talkie, or perhaps like an early model cellphone, the "brick" type. It is a tall rectangular tower, and the top stories curve downward a few degrees, making the building a concave shape. This shape and the fact that the building is covered in highly reflective glass are causing major problems in the local neighborhood. Essentially, the building acts like a curved mirror, focusing the Sun's rays onto a point below, which changes during the day as the Sun moves around the sky, blasting anything in its path with something like a death ray from a science fiction story.

One victim is Mr. Martin Lindsay, who parked his luxury car, a Jaguar XJ, across the street from the building. Returning to his vehicle after lunch, he found that the focused sun rays had caused enormous damage to the car: the wing mirrors, the side panels, and even the Jaguar badge had all been melted. Fortunately for Mr. Lindsay, the building developers agreed to pay for the cost of repairs. Shops in the ray's path have also been damaged. Shopkeepers have reported burns to their carpets and blistering paintwork. A local barber's shop reported a small fire starting on their doormat; the rays even burned a hole in the seat of a bicycle that had been left nearby.

This is not the first time that this building's designer, renowned architect Rafael Vinoly, has caused problems with his creative designs. He designed the Vdara Hotel in Las Vegas with a similar curve that directed the Sun's rays onto the swimming pool deck, melting plastic and singeing sunbathers' hair. The hotel management had to put up extra-large sun umbrellas to shade the area.

The British press, always good with funny headlines, have started to call the building a "fryscraper" or "the Walkie Scorchie." However, the building's developers have taken the problem seriously and have erected a sunshade 37 stories high to deflect the rays and put a stop to the problem. It just proves that although the Sun sustains life on our planet, we should never underestimate its terrible power.

The Miracles of Pythagoras

Pythagoras was a Greek who lived around 500 BC, and as every schoolboy knows, he developed the theory of measuring triangles – in a right-angle triangle, the sum of the length of the two shorter sides will always equal the length of the longer side. This led to the discovery of trigonometry, enabling tall mountains to be measured without having to climb them with a tape measure!

What is less well-known is the strange life of this ancient mathematician and philosopher. He was also a cult leader whose followers worshipped him as a direct descendant of the god Apollo. He forbade his followers to eat meat, becoming the first vegetarian recorded in history. The cult also worshipped numbers with special symbols and prayers. Pythagoras believed that the numbers ten and seven were divine. Reincarnation was also a core belief of the Pythagorean cult. He believed that when a person died, their soul passed into another form, which could be another person or even an inanimate object like a bean. Pythagoras was especially convinced that fava beans were a preferred location for souls to migrate to, and he spent much of his life campaigning to stop people from eating fava beans, which he claimed was "the same as eating your father and mother." Joining the cult of Pythagoras was not an easy task: followers had to give up all possessions and remain completely silent for five years before they were accepted.

Not surprisingly, like many cult leaders, various myths and legends sprung up around him. He was said to be able to tame birds out of the sky with his voice. He claimed to be able to tell the future from divination, examining entrails of sacrificed animals, which was a popular method of prophecy at the time. He was also said to have been seen in two different cities at the same time. In the end, it appears that his strange beliefs were the cause of his death.

The cult of Pythagoras was tolerated for a while in the city of Croton, where it was based, but eventually, the local people got tired of all the eccentric behavior and decided to put a stop to it. Pythagoras managed to escape and was chased to a field of fava beans. Because Pythagoras thought that the beans contained the souls of the dead, he refused to run into the field because it would damage some plants, and his pursuers caught him and killed him. Death by beans – an odd fate for a strange man.

Collective Nouns

A murder of crows, a swarm of bees, a pod of dolphins... have you ever wondered where we get our words for collective nouns?

These words are used to describe groups, and the way we describe them started with a nun towards the end of the fifteenth century. The Book of Saint Albans was written by Sister Juliana Berners and printed in 1486. The terms were originally used as terms for hunting, but some of them passed into everyday language. Many of the terms in the book describe people as well as animals, and many of them aren't used much, if at all, in modern English.

It's not often you'll hear about a school of clerks, feast of brewers, or skulk of thieves. You might, however, hear about a state of princes or a congregation of people, often worshippers. Then there are others that we use every day – we talk about a choir when we want to describe a group of singers, a team when we mean a group of sports or other game players and a crew of sailors or air personnel.

Some of our favorite collective nouns refer to the animal kingdom. Who can resist a tuxedo of penguins, a bask of crocodiles, a parliament of owls, a wisdom of wombats, or a destruction of cats?

Four-footed farm animals may often be described as a herd, while birds are usually referred to as a flock. There are some special words for particular birds that it's fairly hard to guess – you just have to learn them. Some particularly colorful descriptions of birds include a convocation of eagles, a flamboyance of flamingos, and a charm of magpies. And some of those words refer to the noise they make, like squabble of seagull.

When it comes to flying insects, we often describe swarms – think about bees and locusts, for instance. There are special names for some insects, however – we talk about a colony of ants. Colony is also used to describe a group of beavers.

Many birds are referred to as flocks on the ground but have a totally different description when in flight. Geese, for instance, come in flocks or "gaggles" until they fly – at which point they're a "skein." Yes, that is the same word as the one used for yarn.

Plenty of people know how to describe a bunch of flowers, a bouquet or bunch of flowers, and a forest or grove of trees, but did you know it's a bushel of apples and a comb of bananas? Although in practice, many of us say "bunch of bananas" these days.

Do Birds Have Regional Accents?

Birdsong is a delightful part of the soundtrack of our lives in many parts of the world – but did you know that, just like people, birds can have regional accents?

The research all started with British chaffinches. In the 1950s, a behavioral scientist named Peter Marler started noticing that these colorful creatures sounded different depending on the valley. And he started transcribing their songs in longhand, later using a device called a sonogram.

Later, scientists made the discovery that some birds were born knowing how to sing, while others had to learn their songs from adult birds by copying. Sometimes, when copying, the baby birds copying the adults made a mistake. And when this happened, the mistake was then copied in turn by other birds. This evolution of birdsong can happen slowly or quickly.

Birds have two reasons for trying to communicate: they're trying to attract a mate, or they're sending out a warning. It's male songbirds who make all the noise – apparently, females like to hear a familiar accent as it suggests the bird is going to stick around and has a knowledge of the area. There are examples, however, of birds who regularly visit other locations, returning every year, and still manage to attract a mate. In some cases, scientists think that the female doesn't care if the male isn't local, but she does care that the song sounds like one she knows. If a bird mimics a song note for note, this is seen as aggressive behavior, particularly if the creature is from outside the area.

Eventually, it's thought that new baby birds growing up in a certain location will learn both the new dialect caused by the copying error and the longer-standing accent.

New Zealand researchers think that human migration has also affected the ways that birds sound today. When they listened to old recordings of birds called Kokako, the birds used to make metallic-sounding noises that were totally different from anything we now know as bird songs. Some of the bird calls we know today, like the male yellowhammer cry that sounds a little like asking for "a little bit of bread and no cheese," are also likely to evolve in the decades ahead. Some birds can, however, change their dialect depending on where they are – very convenient when they're hunting for a mate.

After emigrants from Britain settled in New Zealand, it's thought their accents changed. Some birds there today, however, still have a "UK" accent, and in this respect, it's not unlike what happens with human settlers as language evolves in different ways. In Canada, for instance, there are words used that have long since fallen out of use in Ireland or Britain. It's something for scientists to think about if they reintroduce birds into areas where they no longer breed - one option is to bring in a group of birds at the same time.

In cities, where noise generally is at high levels, birds sing at a higher pitch. This is thought to be due to the fact that higher-pitched noises travel further as they don't echo off buildings and hard surfaces quite as much, although another interpretation is that birds develop different song pitches so they can all be heard.

And birds aren't the only creatures with local dialects – the same applies to bats and whales.

Have Carrots Always Been Orange?

Ask a random sample of a hundred people to name their favorite vegetable, and we're fairly sure over 60% will say "carrot." They bring color to so many dishes, but did you know that carrots haven't always been orange?

In fact, it wasn't until the late 1500s that growers in what we now call the Netherlands started experimenting with creating orange carrots, probably crossing wild carrots with cultivated ones. Before that, most carrots weren't orange but purple. Very occasionally, you'd see a yellow or a white carrot, but most were a sort of purplish shade.

It's a pigment called anthocyanin that gives purple carrots their color, and it isn't found in white or yellow carrots. Anthocyanin is found in lots of other purple foods like grapes, purple cabbage, blackberries, and purple potatoes. They have plenty of health benefits and are thought to help with diabetes and blood flow, as well as other conditions, including some kinds of cancer.

Purple and red carrots are thought of as Eastern carrots; orange, white, and yellow carrots are associated with the West. Orange carrots are sweeter tasting than purple carrots. It's thought that the ancestors of orange carrots were probably yellow carrots – and they were a mutation.

Orange carrots get that color from a substance called beta-carotene. When we eat carrots, the substances in our stomachs turn beta-carotene into vitamin A. Carrots are good for us, no matter what color, but purple carrots, in particular, have extra benefits that are peculiar to vegetables and fruits of that color – they're also great at helping to combat inflammation. Carrots are packed with nutrients, including vitamins A, C, and B, as well as manganese and potassium. They're also super-versatile – you can eat them raw, roast them, grate them into cakes, add to smoothies, or simply eat them raw. They have even been used as sweeteners.

Many historians think purple carrots were first cultivated around the area we call Afghanistan. Around a third of all the carrots we now eat originate in China. We mainly eat the root part of the carrot plant today, but that wasn't always the case. In Roman times, the belief was that carrot seeds, in particular, were effective in love potions.

You might have heard the myth that carrots are good for your eyesight, especially at night, but this really is just a myth – it was actually a story put about by the government in World War Two to hide the fact that radar was proving so effective - especially at night!

Be careful you don't eat too many carrots, though – you don't want to contract "carotenemia." This can be caused by eating too much food containing beta-carotene. These include yams, sweet potatoes, squash and pumpkins, oranges, mangoes, cantaloupes and apricots, and, of course, orange carrots.

There's no particular health risk, but in carotenemia, the thicker skin on your body can turn orange. This includes your knees and elbows, around the nose, the soles of your feet, and the palms of your hands. Don't worry too much – you would need to eat around ten carrots a day for several weeks to cause this condition.

Where is the Hottest Place on Earth?

In the last few decades, temperatures on Earth have been increasing rapidly – but just where is the hottest place on Earth?

Some of the highest temperatures on the planet have been recorded in Death Valley in California, close to the Nevada border. Although, until recently, there was some debate about what that temperature was.

In July of 1931, a temperature of 131 degrees Fahrenheit (55 degrees Celsius) was on record in Tunisia, but its reliability is in question as the thermometers of the time were not as accurate and precise as the instruments we have now.

There's another tale that the temperature in the Furnace Creek Visitor Center around ten kilometers from Death Valley reached 134.1 degrees Fahrenheit (56.7 degrees Celsius) in July of 1913, but it's thought that it was not recorded for long enough to be reliable.

It was in 1994 that Death Valley was officially declared a National Park. Every year, around one million people visit to experience the extreme heat. Partly due to the heat, there is no cell phone coverage, and due to its remoteness, there are no wired phones either.

One of the most popular spots for tourists is called the Badwater Basin, the lowest point in all of North America. The surface is covered with a thick salt layer; it's 85.5 meters lower than sea level, and there is very little dew or rain in this location.

Astonishingly, Death Valley is extremely popular with tourists, although they are advised to stay in the parts of the park that are well-traveled in case they need help. The authorities also suggest staying in air-conditioned areas, carrying plenty of water, eating small snacks regularly, and visiting viewpoints at higher, cooler elevations. The area has hotels, restaurants, and other facilities that cater to tourists. There's even a swimming pool. In the spring, the area is surprisingly rich with flora, insect life, and birds, including the Road Runner. (Yes, the same type as in the cartoon.). There are even six fish species, including the rare and endangered Devil's Hole Pupfish, which is bright blue.

The temperature in Death Valley broke world records on August 16, 2020, when sensors registered a temperature of 129.9 degrees Fahrenheit (54.4 degrees Celsius). It's a haunting, mysterious landscape where the sands sing if you listen carefully. That's not the only mystery: until recently, scientists were at a loss about how to explain the way some of the rocks move at night.

Other places around the world that are consistently too hot for humans include the Flaming Mountains of China, the Lut Desert of Iran, the Sahara Desert, where water evaporates faster than anywhere else on Earth, and El Azizia in Libya. Even in Las Vegas, temperatures can soar to 47.2 degrees Celsius.

How do people cope with these high temperatures? Well, it's not possible for humans (or other mammals) to endure them for very long. Some options to help humans cope with high temperatures are using bamboo clothing, silk covers on beds and car seats, and rehydration with local berries like mung bean juice in China.

Who Invented the Sandwich?

It's such a versatile option. All you need is some kind of bread or starch-based cover, almost any filling, and presto! You have a convenient, portable meal. You don't need any special utensils. Plus, it's as nutritious – or as luxurious! – as you care to make it.

If you've ever wondered how many sandwiches are eaten in America every day, it's over 300 million. It's one of our most popular snacks. There's even a day to celebrate it – November 3 is National Sandwich Day.

But what genius came up with the idea in the first place? Well, many food historians think the sandwich as we know it was "invented" by politician John Montagu, the fourth Earl of Sandwich, in 1762. It was a historian in England called Edward Gibbon who first wrote about seeing people eating a "Sandwich" in November of that year, although he doesn't mention John Montagu at all, at least not by name.

Montagu was known to be very fond of a game of cards. He hated to be drawn away from the game. One day, he asked his servants to fetch him some food. It had to be something easy to eat; he needed to be able to stay in his seat so he wouldn't miss a second of the game, and it also had to be an item he could eat with just his hands.

The servants brought him two pieces of bread with a serving of meat in between – a sandwich.

By the time of the Revolutionary War in the late 1770s, the sandwich was well-known in England, but it took a little longer to become a popular option in America. We do know there was a recipe for a sandwich in a cookbook in America in 1815. During the Great

Depression of the 1930s, sandwiches were extremely popular. They even had names, like the Reuben or the Sloppy Joe. And in the years since, it's become extremely popular as a quick, simple lunchtime meal. There are countless variations – including, of course, the famous, sustaining, iconic peanut butter and jelly.

Although the sandwich probably got its name because of that long-ago British aristocrat, he was far from the first person to come up with the idea. There is an account from the first century BCE of how a Rabbi known as Hillel the Elder put unleavened matzoh bread, bitter herbs, and Paschal lamb together to make a dish. And there are plenty of accounts of bread rolled with a filling. Over the centuries, there are also mentions in art and literature of agricultural workers often putting cheese or meat in between a couple of hunks of bread for their lunchtime meal.

So, here's to the humble but invaluable sandwich!

The Amazing Moustache Cup

Throughout history, the fashion for sporting a beard, a mustache, sideburns, or all three has changed periodically. And if you've ever seen pictures from the 1870s, you'll know that splendid mustaches were very much in vogue – in the British Army, there were regulations pretty much insisting that soldiers grew a mustache!

Men often spent hours coaxing their facial hair into strictly manicured shapes. Waxing the mustache to keep it in place was something of an occupational hazard when it came to drinking tea. Quite apart from the potential for the tea to stain the hair, there was a real risk of the wax melting into the drink. And if the wax at either side of the glorious facial adornment melted, the curls were in danger of losing their shape.

And so, in the 1870s, as the story goes, a British potter called Harvey Adams came up with a solution: the mustache or mustache cup. This specially designed cup has a ledge inside that's semi-circular in shape. This not-so-secret shelf was a kind of butterfly shape inside the cup, with a carefully placed hole to allow the tea to be drunk.

In America, they were sold all over the place, from Sears to the store that was later known as Macy's, formerly Marshall Field's. Some of the American cups were made of silver plate, but many of the earlier cups, made of pottery, had maker's marks, which suggested they were created in England. They came in different sizes, too – delicate vessels made of porcelain and China, and bigger cups to hold around a pint of liquid, and designed for farmers and working men. Many of them even came with matching saucers and were popular presents.

During World War One, it became much less fashionable to have a mustache, possibly because it made wearing gas masks less effective. From the 1920s to the 1930s, mustaches started becoming less popular, and men were more often clean-shaven.

If you'd like to see mustache cups in real life, you can find them in several museums around the world, including the Norsk Folkemuseum in Oslo, Norway; Wellington County, Ontario; and Bell County Museum. Bell County has the largest publicly held collection of these items in the United States. If you're not able to get to the museums in person to marvel at these relative rarities, many of them have online displays.

Not that mustache cups have been entirely forgotten. At one bar in the Financial District in New York, the manager has sourced several of the items through auction sites, making them quite a talking point. They're used to serve punch made to an old, authentic recipe from the 1870s. Apparently, in modern drinks, that ledge is great for keeping the ice back.

Why Are So Many Wedding Dresses White?

Hundreds of thousands of movies have a wedding as part of the plot – but have you ever wondered why so many brides wear white, in fiction and in real life?

Well, white hasn't always been the color of choice. Historically, for many women, their wedding dress was often either their best dress beforehand or became their best dress after the ceremony. In many parts of the world, white wedding dresses weren't popular historically. In Scandinavia, for instance, black was a popular color.

In the Middle Ages, what a bride wore often reflected the wealth of the family, especially amongst the nobility. Gowns were often bold and bright, made from expensive fabrics, with velvet, silk, and even fur. Brides from less wealthy families would often wear their "Sunday Best" dress.

What members of royalty wear has always had an effect on fashion, but even they didn't choose white very often. Of course, there were exceptions, like Princess Philippa of England. At her "wedding by proxy" in 1406, she wore a white silk tunic and cloak trimmed with fur.

Over 180 years later, in April 1588, when Mary, Queen of Scots, married her first husband, Francis, Dauphin of France, she chose white as it was one of her favorite colors. At this time, for French Queens, white was a mourning color, as it still is in some parts of the world.

It was, however, Queen Victoria who really started the modern trend for white weddings. When she married her cousin Albert in London on February 10, 1840, even her bridesmaids wore white. Her dress featured orange blossom and large amounts of Honiton lace. At the time, the lace industry was in decline, and white was a color that showed off the skill of the lacemakers to dramatic effect.

For the rest of Victoria's reign, the official color of both groomsmen and bridesmaids was white. Some people think white was chosen as it represents purity, but it's also very likely it was chosen to show off the family's wealth since white is such a difficult color to care for. This was certainly the case before modern washing machines. It's also thought white wedding dresses became popular when the new-fangled art of photography came along, as they really stood out in the sepia or black and white images.

In many parts of the world, wedding attire has a tendency to be bright and cheerful. In India and China, wedding dresses are traditionally red to symbolize good luck. In Nigeria, dresses are heavily accessorized and very bright in color, and in Ghana, every family has their own distinctive material pattern. Brides from some cultures, for example, parts of China, like to have both a ceremony in traditional dress and a white wedding.

White doesn't just mean white when it comes to white wedding dresses. Ivory, however, is popular, along with a whole host of other pale colors. Generally, the style of wedding dresses follows the fashion of the time, although since about the late 1960s, some formal gowns have grown more and more extravagant. And these days, it's often really up to the happy couple to decide what suits their personalities and lifestyles. It's now something of a social mistake to wear white at a wedding unless you're actually the bride!

The Country Where No one Ever Worked

Imagine being born in a country where citizens never had to do a day's work in their lives but still had everything they needed. This is what happened in Ancient Sparta, a city-state in Greece. There were several classes of residents in Sparta. Citizens that could trace their hereditary back to earlier times were the first class, the Spartiates.

After that, there were the lower classes consisting of people from other parts of Greece who were known as Helots, who were basically state-owned slaves, and Perioikoi, who were free men but not citizens. The land was divided equally among the citizens, who were actually forbidden to do any labor or work at all. Helots did all the work on the land and provided a living for the Spartiates, not only as agricultural workers but also as household servants. The Perioikoi were the craftsmen and builders who made everything for the citizens.

The only occupation open to Spartan males was being a soldier in the Spartan army, and boys would start their military training as young as seven years old. They all remained in active service until the age of 30, and from then on, they were part of the army reserve. Spartan women were also expected to be educated, mainly in dancing, singing, and poetry, although reading and writing were also taught, and Sparta was the only place in the world at that time that treated women as equals to men.

Although at first glance, the life of a Spartan citizen seems enviable, never having to work, in reality, it was a very hard life in the Spartan army. They were fed enough to live but were still hungry so they would never become fat and lazy. Training was tough, and many did not survive it. Also, they were expected to give their lives rather than surrender in battle. Spartan mothers would say to their sons as they handed them their soldier's shield, "Either come back with it or on it." In other words, come back victorious or with your body carried on your shield. A young Spartan could be forgiven for thinking he would just rather get a job!

The First Strike in History

Around 3,000 years ago, about the year 1150 BC, Egypt was a very peaceful kingdom. In fact, social harmony was seen as most valuable. The pharaoh was always conscious of the fact that it was his duty to maintain harmony throughout the land, making sure every person was cared for, that no one suffered unduly, that the crops were managed correctly, and that the country's borders were secure. This idea of the value of harmony was known as the principle of Ma'at, and in fact, it applied to all inhabitants of Egypt – all were expected to live in peace and harmony.

This harmonious peace began to fall apart at one point by the very first recorded labor strike in history. This had its origins in several battles against invaders from the sea, who attacked Egyptian coastal areas and tried to invade inland. Under the Pharaoh Ramesses III, known as Ramesses the Great, the sea invaders were defeated but at great cost in terms of men and resources. The royal treasury was drained, and as a result, the pharaoh decided to raise taxes while, at the same time, he toured the country and refurbished temples and monuments. The cost of his royal entourage as it went around the country was an enormous expense, as was the rebuilding and renovations he ordered to public buildings. This drained the treasury even further.

The pharaoh believed he had dedicated his life to the service of his country, and as he approached his 30th year on the throne, a grand jubilee was planned to celebrate with the most lavish and expensive ceremonies. The cost of this took nearly all the remaining Royal resources, and as a result, salaries to public workers were delayed.

One of these situations was the workers who were building the pharaoh's tomb and mortuary tombs for other Egyptian nobles at a necropolis, an area like a huge cemetery at a place called Deir Al

Medina. The workers' pay was late on several occasions, and they complained to local officials, who ignored the problem and instead concentrated on preparing for the grand jubilee. The workers waited for 18 days after their official pay date, then they downed tools and marched into the city shouting, "We are hungry." They then staged a sit-in at one of the temples and refused to continue working.

The local officials had no idea how to deal with this situation because nothing like this had ever happened before. The concept of Ma'at applied throughout the land from pharaoh to farmer and was never before disturbed like this. Workers rising up and making demands was an impossible situation – it just could not happen. So, with no other ideas of what to do, officials ordered sweet pastries to be delivered to the striking workers so that they would be happy again and go back to work. But this did not work, and the striking workers next went to the grain storehouses and temples to demand their payment. The chief of police was called, and he negotiated a settlement for back pay between the workers and local officials.

After that, all was quiet for a while. The jubilee celebrations went ahead, and everything seemed back to normal. However, after the jubilee, the workers' pay was again delayed, and this time, the striking workers blocked the entrance to the Valley of the Kings, so people could not enter and pay respects to the dead or, indeed, bury any relatives. This time, the strike was not just about pay but about the principle of Ma'at that the pharaoh had failed to uphold. He was supposed to take care of all his people, and in the case of the tomb workers, he had not done so. The strikes continued for over three years until officials finally organized ways to ensure salaries were paid on time.

News of this spread throughout the kingdom, and over the following centuries, other groups went on strike when they felt their harmony was being disturbed. This was the very first strike by workers in recorded history, but certainly not the last.

UFOs Over Nuremburg

We tend to think of sightings of Unidentified Flying Objects (UFOs) as a relatively modern phenomenon, and the inspirations behind science fiction writers whose stories about visitors from space further convinced people that strange lights in the sky were spaceships from another planet.

Actually, UFO sightings have been recorded as far back as 1400 BC in Ancient Egypt. In Roman times, from 250 BC to 75 BC, the historians at that time noted strange occurrences, shapes like ships of metal objects appearing in the heavens and then vanishing. Such phenomena have been seen in every century from the early days through the Middle Ages and right up to the present day. Scientists are always quick to find rational explanations for these, but there are some that just cannot be explained in terms of the natural world around us.

One such case happened in the skies over the city of Nuremberg, Germany, in 1561. The residents of the city claimed to have seen not just one but many objects in the sky, and they appeared to be fighting. A newspaper that was printed as a broadsheet at the time and which is now on display in a local museum describes the mass sighting of celestial phenomena. The witnesses said they observed hundreds of cylindrical and spherical objects moving erratically overhead, and they appeared to be fighting each other until most of them fell to Earth, where they burned up in clouds of smoke. At the end of the battle, a large black triangular object, which they described as like the head of a spear, appeared in the sky and later seemed to crash-land outside the city limits, although the site of the crash was not found. At that time, the strange event was given a religious interpretation. People in those days knew nothing about aliens, space, or even other planets. It was believed to be a warning from God that the residents of the city would be punished for their sins and that they should repent.

The event has been much studied and analyzed over the years, including by scientists, philosophers, and psychologists, notably Carl Jung, who all believe the cause was a natural phenomenon like ice crystals floating around in the dawn sky or even a case of mass hysteria. Regardless of the modern explanations, the people of Nuremberg "saw what they saw," and although an alien invasion is the least likely explanation, it can never be ruled out. You can never be too sure – remember, the truth is out there!

The Man Who Nearly Lost FedEx in a Card Game

The worldwide shipping and courier company FedEx was started in the 1970s by a Yale University graduate, Mr. Fred Smith, a few years after graduation. The company was based on a case study he wrote as a student. In the case study, he wrote about how shipping companies should be able to deliver packages a lot faster if they changed the way they operated. However, Fred's professor at Yale did not think his ideas would work, and the paper was given a 'C' grade.

Fred Smith graduated from Yale, joined the Marine Corps, and completed two tours of duty in Vietnam.

When he returned to the U.S., he bought into a company that manufactured aviation parts, and here he was frustrated by how long it took to send out customer's orders. He decided to put to use the strategies he had discussed in his paper at Yale. Fortunately, some investors at the time could see that his ideas had merit, and he was able to raise millions of dollars in capital to start his own shipping company. He called it Federal Express and shortened it to FedEx since it was an express service across federal and state lines.

The company started operating in 1973 and quickly expanded – possibly too quickly. The cost of operations also increased mainly due to rising fuel costs: in the mid-seventies, a number of world crises sent the price of petroleum-based products sky-rocketing, and since FedEx relied on fast, efficient transport, he could barely keep up with the costs of running fleets of vehicles 24/7. With his cash reserves fast disappearing, Fred went back to his investors, but they were now very cautious and refused to give him any more money to keep the company afloat. Fred next visited his contacts at General Dynamics, a large aerospace company in Virginia that he had dealt with many times, but again, they refused to invest.

Fred had only $5,000 left in the bank, and his company was facing bankruptcy. As a last desperate act, Fred stopped off at Las Vegas on the way back from Virginia and sat down at the blackjack tables with his last $5,000. This time, luck was in his favor, and he won $27,000. He left the table and immediately wired the money back to his company to keep it going and pay the bills for another month.

During that month, luck smiled on Fred again, and after knocking on every door he could find, he managed to get some investors to put in $11 million to put FedEx back on its feet. By 1976, the company revenue was in the order of $75 million, and the company went public, listing shares on the stock market. In 1983, the company reported a turnover of $1 billion, and by 2020, this had grown to $69.7 billion.

Fred Smith still runs the company and has said that winning the $27,000 gave him a sign that everything would get better, and he was right. Gambling with the company's last $5,000 could be seen as a risk and maybe crazy. Fred Smith said, "No business school would recommend gambling as a financial strategy, but sometimes it pays to be a little bit crazy." It certainly paid off for Fred Smith and FedEx.

The Strange Sport of Ferret Legging

You only have to look in something like the Guinness Book of Records to see that, along with the more usual athletic events, there have been many unusual and bizarre sporting achievements setting records for endurance and prowess. Some of them defy the imagination – for example, the greatest number of clothes pegs that a person can attach to their face – achievements that make you ask yourself, "Why would anyone want to do this in the first place, let alone do it competitively?"

One such sport, if it can be called a sport, is ferret-legging. Simply put, men put ferrets down their trousers and see how long they can hold out before giving in.

This was believed to originate in the days when most land was owned by private landlords, men of wealth and title, and poachers would use ferrets to assist with hunting rabbits and other game. The ferrets would be tied to a leash or string and forced into a rabbit warren, where the vicious little creatures would later emerge with a prize rabbit for the poacher's dinner table or to sell in the market.

If spotted, the poacher would try to hide the ferret in his trousers, which was not an easy thing to do since the ferret would be alarmed and start scratching and biting. Still, the poacher had to hide the ferret for as long as possible because being caught with a ferret would mark them as carrying out illegal activities, stealing game from the landowner's property, and punishable by law.

Thus started the contest of ferret legging, mainly in the north of England around Yorkshire. Men would first tie a string around the bottom of their trouser legs to stop the ferrets from escaping and would then see who could hold a ferret in their trousers the longest.

Strangely enough, this still happens in the present day, with regular contests held in pubs around Yorkshire. The record in 1972 was 40 seconds, which may not seem a very long time but would probably be an eternity for a man with a snapping, scratching, scrambling animal around sensitive parts of his body.

However, the limits of human endurance have not yet been reached, and the world champion set an amazing time of over 5 hours with two ferrets down his trousers, and he also played a game of darts at the same time. Ferret legging is not just restricted to Yorkshire; it also takes place in Canada at agricultural shows and in Australia. It was tried in America, where various commentators called it "the most baffling sport" and "the world's dumbest sport." It is hard to disagree with either description, and the words of an extreme sportsman say it all when he was quoted as saying, "After trying ferret legging, falling down a mountain doesn't seem so bad at all."

Are Parallel Universes Real?

We have all seen movies and TV shows about people who encounter a parallel universe and find another version of themselves and their world, but everything is a little different. Of course, it's all fantasy, just science fiction. But sometimes science fiction becomes science fact – remember, Jules Verne wrote stories about men landing on the moon about 100 years before it actually happened.

Well, recent scientific theories indicate that there could be, and probably are, parallel universes. Some of which are perhaps exactly like ours but slightly different. It is all to do with astrophysics, string theory, and quantum mechanics, which are almost impossible to understand unless you are at the intellectual level of a nuclear physicist. But luckily, there is a simple way to explain it.

We know the universe is infinite. It just keeps going through space and never ends. Everything is made out of atoms, and the theory of quantum mechanics states that there are only a fixed number of atoms, which keep repeating in different combinations throughout the universe. This is like having a deck of cards; you can put the cards in many different combinations running into the thousands, but you only have 52 cards, so eventually, the combinations will repeat. The latest theory is the same with universes – sooner or later, the atoms will repeat themselves in a similar pattern to our universe, and there will be another universe with the same planets, the same Earth, and the same people as us!

Where the difference comes in is that in any universe, we will still have the freedom to make choices, so although you may be the same person, your life might be completely different if you make different life decisions in a parallel universe. In a parallel universe, you may be a billionaire, or you could be homeless, living on the street. In fact, you might exist in a number of different universes, leading a different life in each one.

This seems mind-boggling, but unfortunately, we will never actually get to see a parallel universe – we are talking about the infinity of space, and if there is another Earth out there, it will be an infinite number of light years away. So, until they invent space travel at the speed of light, it looks like this is the only universe we will ever know.

The Cottingley Fairies

Children love the idea of fairies, and fairy stories have been told to children throughout time, but have you ever wondered where the idea for the existence of fairies first came from? Maybe fairies are real and always have been. Perhaps it's just that we have never actually seen them.

That all changed in the village of Cottingley in the north of England in 1917.

Two children, 9-year-old Frances, and 16-year-old Elsie, often played by a small stream at the back of their garden and were regularly scolded by their parents for coming home with wet feet and muddy clothes. They always told their parents that they had been playing with the fairies, and this explanation was met with smiles and chuckles. One day, however, Elsie asked her father to borrow a camera so she could prove that the fairies were real. Her father let her borrow his camera, expecting to see just pictures of the children playing together. Thirty minutes later, Elsie returned and gave the camera back to her father, Arthur, who developed the picture himself from the plate used in the old-fashioned version of photography.

What he saw was Frances sitting by a bush on which four fairy-like creatures were dancing. Arthur knew his daughter Elsie was very artistic, so he assumed it was a fake and dismissed it as a prank.

A couple of months later, Elsie borrowed the camera again and, this time, took a photo of a gnome with wings, about a foot tall, holding hands with Frances. Arthur became annoyed at what he believed to be a trick, and he refused to lend them the camera again.

It would have been forgotten about, except that two years later, there was a spiritualist meeting in Bradford that Elsie's mother attended. She showed the photos of the fairies to the person holding the meeting, who passed them on to a leading member of the society, Edward Gardner. Gardner was very interested and visited Cottingley himself. He took two cameras as presents for the two girls and asked them to take some more pictures of the fairies, which they did, producing three more photos of themselves playing with fairies in the garden.

The pictures were published in several magazines, and although some critics insisted they must be faked, no one could see how it was done, and they were generally accepted as real. Even the great Arthur Conan Doyle, author of the Sherlock Holmes stories, was interested and believed they were genuine. Conan Doyle wrote an article for the Strand magazine about them and subsequently was contacted by a number of people saying they had also seen fairies. But, up until then, they had not told anyone for fear of being laughed at.

Finally, in a television interview in the early 1980s, the girls, who were grown up, admitted the photographs had been faked, using cardboard cut-outs from a children's book of fairy stories. They both said that they wanted to tell the truth earlier, but so many people had believed them they just decided to keep quiet.

So, if your children tell you they play with the fairies at the bottom of the garden, don't bother with a camera – sometimes pictures don't tell the complete truth.

The Travels of Marco Polo – Real or Fake?

The name Marco Polo has historically been linked to great voyages of discovery that even inspired Christopher Columbus to embark on his travels. Tales of the Silk Road to the Far East and China and stories of emperors and great marvels, all recounted in his book "The Travels of Marco Polo." But questions have always been raised: did he actually travel, or was it all a work of fiction?

Marco Polo was born in Venice, Italy, in 1254 into a family of wealthy merchants and traders. When he was 17 years old, he traveled with his father and uncle to Asia on a trading expedition; they had previously traveled there several years before, but this time, they did not return to Venice for 24 years, spending 17 of those years in China. Marco apparently developed a strong relationship with the Emperor of China and even worked for him in his administration. The Polo family returned to Venice in 1295 with a great fortune in gold and jewels to find that the city-state of Venice was at war with Genoa, another state. Marco, with his new wealth, built and fitted out a warship, which he personally commanded and went to fight the Genoans, but the forces of Venice were defeated. Marco was taken prisoner and held for ransom.

In prison, he met a writer, Rustichello, and he told the writer all his stories of his travels. Rustichello later wrote the book "The Travels of Marco Polo" based on their conversations, and when the book was published, it became a best-seller, popular throughout Europe. When Marco was eventually released from prison, he returned to Venice and never left home again, dying there in 1324 at the age of 60.

In the book, it tells how Marco traveled the Silk Road to China, where he met the Emperor of China, Kublai Khan, in his residence in what is now Beijing. He also traveled extensively through China and the northeast to Mongolia, visiting Tibet and Burma. He claimed to have visited Japan, where he saw red oyster pearls and a great temple made of solid gold. However, when the Polos decided to return home, the emperor would not let them leave, so they had to stay in China for many years until they found a way to leave by subterfuge.

At that time, Persia, modern-day Iraq, was ruled by Mongols, and the emperor of Persia arranged to marry one of the daughters of the emperor of China. The Polos convinced the Chinese emperor to let them travel with the bride to accompany her to the wedding, and the emperor agreed. They went by sea, visiting Indonesia and Sri Lanka, and when they arrived in Persia, the Polos took another ship bound for Venice.

But over the centuries, there have been many who believe the book is a work of fiction and that Marco Polo never traveled to China. There are many things omitted from his descriptions of Chinese life that he should have noticed – tea, for example, which was unknown in Italy at that time, eating with chopsticks, and the practice of foot-binding. One glaring omission is that there was no mention of the Great Wall of China, which he could hardly fail to notice. Other errors include the fact that red pearl oysters are not found in Japanese waters, and the golden palace he described was built long after he left the country.

Marco Polo also claimed to have brought pasta to Italy from China, where wheat noodles had been eaten for centuries, but it is now known that, in fact, the Arabs who colonized Sicily brought pasta with them from the Middle East. He said he visited the city of Hangzhou and found it full of canals like Venice, with 12,000 bridges. This ridiculous claim was disproven by a later traveler who could find only about 350 bridges. He described the palace of Kublai Khan as having a dining hall that could accommodate 6,000 people and the palace had a wall 32 miles long around it, but there are no records of a palace this size. Also, there are no records of many of the cities he claimed to have visited. The names of the places are unknown.

Even during his own lifetime, Marco Polo was considered a liar and a fabricator by the Italian people who knew him, but to the end of his life, he maintained it was all true. On his death bed, he was asked by his friends to confess to having made it all up, to free his soul from sin, but he told them, "I have not written even half of what I have seen in my life."

The Photo of the Loch Ness Monster

There may have been, as some folk believe, a prehistoric creature living in Loch Ness in Scotland since the days of the dinosaurs, but sightings of the legendary beast only date back to 1933. A new road had been built along the shore, making it easy for tourists and locals to visit the lake, and shortly after the road was completed, a young couple walking around the lake reported seeing a huge animal swimming in the Loch. Their story was printed in a local paper, the Inverness Courier and this was the start of the tale of the Loch Ness Monster.

A well-known big game hunter called Marmaduke Wetherell was hired by a London newspaper to investigate the claim, but after spending some time at the Loch, he did not see it. However, he did find what he said were its footprints – some large tracks in the mud near the lake. Researchers from the Natural History Museum went to have a look and decided they were fake, made by something like an elephant or hippo foot, probably from an umbrella stand of the sort a big game hunter might have in his home. Caught out and publicly embarrassed as a fraud, Wetherell left quietly and disappeared from view.

Some months later, there was a new sensation at Loch Ness. A surgeon, Doctor Robert Wilson, was driving past the lake when he saw something in the water, so he stopped to have a look. Luckily, he had a camera with him, and he took a photograph of what appeared to be a sea monster, like a dinosaur, swimming through the Loch. This caused a huge controversy when the photo was published in the press, with many skeptics claiming it to be fake and many others declaring it was proof of a monster in the Loch. Naturally, after that, many people came forward claiming to have seen the monster, but unfortunately, no other photographs were taken to prove their claims.

The truth was finally revealed. In 1994, shortly before his death at the age of 90, a man named Christian Spurling confessed to having a part in a hoax. He had been asked by Wetherell, his stepfather, to build something like a sea monster. He used a miniature submarine and made a serpent's head with a long neck to fit on the submarine, and this is what was photographed by Doctor Wilson, who was also part of the conspiracy. The fake monster was only three feet long, but because there was nothing in the background to compare it to, only the waters of the Loch, it looked a lot bigger in the photo. The whole plan was dreamed up by Marmaduke Wetherell in revenge for his humiliation over the "hippo footprints," and his friend Wilson and his stepson Spurling helped him. His stepson remembered him saying, "They want a monster? Okay, we will give them one," and so he did.

Is there really a Loch Ness monster? Many still believe, but the only photograph ever taken turned out to be fake, so no one really knows to this day.

A Real Traveler in Time

The great physicist Albert Einstein actually proved that, in theory, at least, traveling in time is possible. The theory is that if you travel in space faster than the speed of light, time will slow down for you so that one minute of your time may be one year of Earth time so that when you return to Earth after a month, you would be almost the same age as when you left, but it would be many years in the future on Earth. But it only works one way; there is no theory that suggests it is possible to go back in time, only forward.

Traveling from the past into the future seemed to become a reality one day in 1950. According to all accounts, a man suddenly appeared in the middle of New York's Times Square. He was said to look like he was panicking, and he ran across the street, where he was hit by a car and died at the scene.

His body was taken to the local morgue and examined. He was wearing old-fashioned, Victorian-style clothes, and he had a number of strange items in his pockets, including:

– $70 in old banknotes

– A copper token for a 5-cent beer

– A bill for the care of a horse from a stable on Lexington Avenue

– A medal for coming third in a three-legged race

– Business cards with the name Rudolf Hentz with an address on Fifth Avenue

When police checked the address, they found it was a business, but there was a Rudolf Hentz in an old phone book, so the police tried to trace him through that. They discovered that Hentz had died in 1940, but his widow was still alive, so the police officer went to see her. She had been married to Rudolf Hentz junior, a man whose father, also named Rudolf Hentz, disappeared suddenly in 1876 after going out for a walk. The police officer checked the missing person files that still existed in the City Hall archives and found the description exactly matched the man who had appeared in 1950 in his age, his clothing, and his appearance. The case was marked unsolved – was this man a time traveler by accident? The story spread around the world and was accepted as an example of the paranormal, like alien abductions. But what really happened?

The Rudolf Hentz story had been widely accepted since the 1950s, and in 2000, a paranormal researcher, Chris Aubeck, finally decided to check it out. Aubeck found the original source of the story – a science fiction short story written and published in 1951 by author Jack Finney. Two years later, it was reprinted in a booklet issued by a group called Borderland, which promoted the idea of the paranormal, and it was presented as fact, not fiction. Through this booklet, the story began to circulate around Europe and around the world, where it was accepted as reality. Actually, many people around the world still believe the story of the accidental time traveler really happened. Time travel may happen one day in the future, but not this time – it was just a good story.

How Reading Affects Your Brain

Ever since books were first created, learning to read has become one of our most basic and most important skills. Not being able to read, to be illiterate, is to be cut off not only from the world of literature but from most of the technology of the modern world, which all involves reading at some level. Text messages, emails, Facebook, Twitter, and news websites all require the ability to read to understand and take part in them. Thankfully, all children in Western societies are taught to read at an early age and in most other areas of the world except for the most primitive tribes.

One sad fact, though, is that many people do not make full use of this skill and spend time only on smartphones and computers or watching TV, without ever really picking up a book and reading it. Apart from the wonderful resources available to students through textbooks and non-fiction books, the world of fiction books gives someone access to some of the greatest experiences they will ever have as they open their imagination and explore the creations of hundreds of thousands of great writers over the centuries, from Homer to Dickens, from tales of Hercules and Jason and the Argonauts to modern-day stories of adventure and thrills.

More importantly, scientists have been investigating how reading fiction books can change the brain. Each person's brain might be different according to their reading habit, which can affect certain parts of the brain, especially in the early years of growth. Reading a story puts us in the mind and body of the chief character, the one telling the story or the one the story is about. Our brain simulates the sensations and movement of the character and changes the brain's neurons so that we learn what it is like to be that person and how they feel, and we practically feel the same way. This experience has been found to leave impressions on the brain and strengthen the networks that enable us to understand others better, increasing what is known as our Emotional IQ. It also changes parts of the brain involved in language and speech, helping us to speak more clearly and helps us to have more complex thought patterns.

Scientists experimented with scanning the brains of students using an MRI scanner to check brain activity while the students were reading a book of fiction by writer Robert Harris about Pompeii. They noticed increased activity in the regions of the brain most connected with language and with visual concepts as if the students were actually not just reading but were in the story in real life. This brain activity continued after they finished reading and seemed to build stronger abilities in the brain to do with learning and memory.

What this all tells us is that reading, as well as being an enjoyable and entertaining hobby, helps the brain to grow and develop in many ways and increases practical intelligence. This is of great benefit to everyone and will also help people avoid things like dementia and Alzheimer's as they get older. When we read a book, we become part of the story as if we were really there. The last words on this can go to George RR Martin, who wrote the Game of Thrones books:

"A reader lives a thousand lives before they die..."

When Pie Eating was Banned

Everybody loves a pie – apple pie, peach pie, steak pie, anything wrapped in a pastry case is a good pie, and pies have been popular for centuries. One story says that pies were invented by miners' wives who used to wrap up their husbands' lunch, meat, and vegetables in a pastry casing and drop them down the mine shafts for their husbands to catch. Whatever the origins, they have always been a well-liked type of food, and the first reference to them as food items, called "pyes," appeared in England in the 12th century.

But there was a time in English history when not only was the pie unpopular, but it was actually against the law to be found eating a pie. It happened after the civil war in England when Royalists who supported the monarchy of King Charles I fought against the Parliamentarians led by Oliver Cromwell, who wanted England to be ruled by an elected parliament, not by a king. Cromwell's army won, and Oliver Cromwell led a parliament that ruled England from 1644 to 1658 until the monarchy was restored and King Charles II took over the throne.

Cromwell did not dislike pies, but as a strict puritan, he did not hold with people enjoying themselves in what he called "sinful pagan pleasures." His plan was to ban Christmas in England because he believed it was a pagan festival based on the old Roman mid-winter feast of Saturnalia. As a part of his beliefs, he decided that pies, mainly mince pies, a sugary treat, were included in the list of pagan pleasures and should be banned because they were traditionally eaten at Christmas time.

To avoid people getting around the law by putting fillings other than sweet mince in the pies, he banned all pies for the whole year. But if people want to eat pies, it is very difficult to stop them, and like the prohibition against alcohol in the U.S., pie making and pie eating went underground. There were secret bakers and pie-makers who sold their wares on the black market, no doubt at inflated prices, and there may even have been secret gatherings of rebellious folk who got together to guiltily eat their pies before the authorities arrived to arrest them.

Eventually, in 1658, the monarchy was restored, and in 1660, two years after Cromwell's death, the bans on pies and on Christmas were reversed, and once again, all of England could celebrate the holiday season with a feast, including many mince pies.

Edison Never Invented Anything

Thomas Alva Edison is credited with many inventions, including the light bulb, the phonograph, and the motion picture camera. In total, he held patents on 1093 inventions, but in fact, he didn't really invent any of them. What he actually did, and what was the driving force behind many of the inventions we use today, was the creation of a scientific research center, or what could be called an industrial research laboratory, where he worked with a team of people who developed existing inventions and looked for new ones.

The only thing that Edison really invented was the concept of acquiring new technology, hiring near-geniuses, and attracting investment capital to make it all work for the general public. More than anything else, Edison was a businessman, an "ideas" man, and an excellent marketer.

The lightbulb is a great example of Edison's genius. It was Humphrey Davy in England who originally found that when electric current passed through thin wires, the wires heated up and began to glow, giving off a light. But all the wires that he used burned out too quickly, and it was another English scientist, Warren de la Rue, who found a material that would last longer and burn brighter if sealed in a vacuum tube, but he used platinum, which was way too expensive to be ever used by ordinary people. This is where Edison came in with his research laboratory. By using stronger filaments and better but cheaper thin glass vacuums, Edison created a lightbulb that lasted a long time at a price that could be commercially successful.

Another good example is the telephone, which was invented in 1876 by Alexander Graham Bell. Edison's team took it in 1878 and added a carbon filament microphone, which would enable better clarity, especially for long-distance calls. A similar project was the phonograph, which Edison developed into a machine that could record and play back sounds, inscribing the sound waves onto a spinning wax disc.

So maybe Edison did not really invent anything, but he was able to take existing inventions and make them better, and make them accessible and useful to the general public, and without his work and that of his team, we would not have many of the modern conveniences we see around us today.

The Curse of Tamerlane

Temur Gurkani, known as Tamerlane, was a Mongol emperor and a descendant of the great Genghis Khan. Tamerlane controlled a vast army that included people from many nations and ethnicities, and over his life, he invaded and conquered most of the ancient world from China through Central Asia, even Africa and Europe. It is estimated that he and his army killed over 17 million people, which was 5% of the world population at that time, so naturally, every country feared him.

He died in 1405 and was laid to rest in a tomb in Samarkand, a city in Uzbekistan, at a place called Gur-Emir. His body was undisturbed for more than 500 years until 1941, when Russian anthropologists asked permission to excavate the tomb for historical reasons. Uzbekistan, at that time, was part of the U.S.S.R., and so they were allowed to begin work. However, the local people, the Uzbeks, were very concerned and complained that their history was being ravaged and that Tamerlane should be left in peace.

Also, they claimed that there was a curse on the tomb that would release a terrible disaster on the world if it was opened. Tamerlane himself had laid the curse, saying, "Whoever disturbs my tomb will unleash an invader more terrible than I."

Despite the protests, the Russian expedition went ahead, and the tomb was opened on June 20, 1941. Tamerlane's curse seemed to come true – within two days, on June 22, 1941, Hitler declared war on Russia, and his Nazi armies invaded the country in Operation Barbarossa. The expedition was quickly wound up, and Tamerlane's remains were flown to Moscow for further study. The Russian leader at that time, Josef Stalin, was a superstitious man; he had heard about the curse of Tamerlane, and he believed it.

After a year of a terrible battle between Russian and German forces in Stalingrad, and as a symbolical sign of hope, Stalin decided to send Tamerlane's remains back to Samarkand, but first, he ordered the plane carrying the remains to circle over Stalingrad several times before flying back to Uzbekistan, where Tamerlane was reburied in his tomb with full honors, and the tomb sealed up once again.

Whether by coincidence or by the curse being lifted, the battle of Stalingrad ended a month later with a Russian victory, although it had caused the death of over 2 million soldiers and civilians – an achievement of which only Tamerlane would be proud.

The Y2K Bug

We tend to think of ourselves as modern, sophisticated people, and while we all may not understand everything about the latest technology, we are generally comfortable with using its products, such as smartphones, tablets, and laptop computers. However, there was a time, not so long ago, when the world became scared of a great disaster linked to computer technology, and there was general concern and panic that it would mean almost the end of civilization. The problem was known as the Millennium Bug, or the Y2K bug, the Y for Year, and the K for thousand. So, it was short for the Year 2000 bug, with "bug" being computer slang for something in a program that will cause a problem.

When computers were first designed in the 1960s, to save space on the limited-size discs, the programmers used just the two last numbers in their coding, for example, dropping the 19 off the date 1960 and just using the 60. All went well for the next 40 years, until 1999 when computer experts became concerned that there would be problems with the date of the year 2000. In its current format, the date would be shown simply as 00, and they started to think that computers would not recognize this as a date and may malfunction or just stop working completely.

Just about everything in the world was either controlled by a computer or used a computer in its operating system. If they malfunctioned, electric grids would shut down, planes would fall out of the sky, cars and other vehicles would become useless, and worst of all, the missile guidance systems that the superpowers used for nuclear weapons would become uncontrollable. Predictions were that the world would be plunged back into the dark ages and disaster would overtake the planet. This was a real fear, and many people turned to “survivalist” conspiracies, buying weapons to defend their homes when law and order broke down and stocking their basements with dried and canned goods. Many computer experts found it to be a very profitable time, as large and small companies wanted programmers to fix their systems so that it would not affect them so much, rewriting date programs to allow for the change of the century.

So, what happened when the day finally came and the new millennium dawned across the planet? Yes, there were problems:

- Bus ticket machines in Australia failed to operate
- In Japan, some models of mobile phones were deleting messages automatically
- In France and the U.S., some digital clocks showed the date as 01-01-1910
- In Delaware, lottery ticket machines stopped working

These were just some of the many small issues that affected computer systems at the start of the year 2000, but most systems just carried on as normal, either unaffected by the date change or because they had been reprogrammed in advance. The world did not end with the dawn of the new century, but it was a warning that maybe we rely on technology just a bit too much.

More Chess Moves Than Atoms in the Universe

What are the most numerous things we can think of? Maybe it is the number of grains of sand on all the beaches in the world. Maybe it is the number of stars in the universe. Whatever you might think of, it is unlikely to be how many moves you can make on a board game.

Chess is a complicated game with different pieces allowed to move in different ways across a board, and it has been played for centuries.

While it is relatively easy to learn how to play chess, learning how to win at chess is an entirely different matter, requiring skill and concentration learned over many years of practice. But actually, the true complexity of chess lies not in the strategies required to be a successful chess player but in the number of possible moves a player can make with his pieces.

The game starts with the player playing the white pieces, moving one piece. His opponent, with the black pieces, then moves one piece. Believe it or not, after those first two moves, there are then 400 possible moves a player can make. After the next three moves, there are then 8,902 possible ways a piece can be moved on the board.

A mathematician, Claude Shannon, has calculated that after each player has moved pieces 5 times, there are 69,352,859,712,417 possible moves that the two players can make from there over the 64 squares on the board with the 32 chess pieces, and this is called the Shannon number. If the game lasts for 40 moves, this number will get so big it is almost possible to calculate.

It has been estimated that the number of possible chess moves is greater than the number of all the hairs on the head of every human on

Earth, more than every grain of sand on all the beaches of the world, and more than the number of atoms in the observable universe. So, if you are a chess player, next time you sit down to play, remember you are playing the most complex game not only in the world but in the entire universe.

“Let Them Eat Cake”

There have been many times in history when a monarch or a leader has met with disaster simply because they lost touch with their people. In modern parlance, they “failed to read the room.” This was certainly the case in the 1790s in France when the population grew tired of being ruled by a royal family who were extravagant in their wealth while so many of the ordinary people lived in poverty and starvation.

At that time, the country was ruled by King Louis XVI and his wife, Queen Marie Antoinette. Although they saw themselves as kind rulers who genuinely cared for people, they were reluctant to change the way of life and traditions of the French monarchy that had existed for hundreds of years, and although many senior members of the government wanted reform of the laws to make them fairer for everyone, Louis and Marie-Antoinette resisted all requests for change, instead building great palaces and gardens around Paris and in Versailles which were only for their own use.

In 1789, the people had enough of their perceived tyranny, and a crowd in Paris stormed the Bastille, the central prison, on June 14, freeing all the prisoners. The Revolutionary National Assembly was formed, marking the start of the French Revolution. At first, the Assembly tried to work with the king and queen and abolish practices that had existed since the Middle Ages, like the system of feudalism, where most land was owned by lords and the people who worked the land were regarded almost as slaves.

The Assembly also wanted to limit the powers of the monarchy so that the king and queen were figureheads without real authority.

But Louis and his wife refused to change and tried to raise enough followers from around France and Europe to put down the revolution. They refused to accept that the country was in need of change, and a defining moment came when Marie-Antoinette was approached by the Assembly to release money from the royal treasury to feed the starving population of Paris with the request, "The people are hungry, they have no bread." Marie-Antoinette famously replied, "Then let them eat cake." This caused a huge outcry because, of course, if people were so poor that they could not buy bread, they certainly could not afford to buy cake!

Eventually, the revolutionary leaders grew frustrated with trying to deal with the king and queen, and they organized the storming of the Tuileries Palace in Paris, taking the king and queen prisoner on August 10, 1792. They both remained in prison while the Assembly argued about what to do with them and eventually, it was decided that they could never go free since they may raise an army against the revolution. Finally, in 1793, they were both executed by guillotine under the banner of the French Revolution, which read, "Liberte, Equalite, Fraternite." Sadly, if the king and queen had accepted those words and changed their rule, they would have lived to see old age instead of dying too soon in the Place de Concorde in Paris.

The Curse of the Pharaohs

In ancient times, most people were either cremated when they died or buried in simple graves. But some people who were believed to be especially important were laid in tombs, often complete with the same objects with which they surrounded themselves in life. In those days, unscrupulous thieves made a good living from robbing graves, and this was especially the case in Egypt in the time of the pharaohs.

Conscious of this, it was common for a pharaoh or other powerful and wealthy persons to put a curse on the tomb so that misfortune and death would occur to anyone who entered the tomb to rob it. While superstitious people believed in the power of the curse, many grave robbers were brave enough to ignore it and went ahead with their thieving. History does not record much in the way of any curses coming true, but there was one occasion when there certainly seemed to be something unnatural happening after a tomb was opened.

In 1922, Howard Carter, an Egyptologist, was on an expedition to the Valley of the Kings in Egypt in the Nile Valley, together with Lord Carnarvon, his sponsor who paid for the expedition. In November of that year, Carter located what he believed to be the entrance to the tomb of Tutankhamun, a boy king who had died in 1323 BC, one of the last of the Egyptian pharaohs. By February of the following year, Carter and his team had unsealed the door, and the tomb was opened for the first time in over 3,000 years.

Carter and Carnarvon entered the tomb and were astounded to find it intact, with riches and treasures beyond their expectations. Most of the abundant wealth was in a side room, the treasury room, and it has been reported that there was a statue of the God Anubis by the door. Anubis, the God of death, was represented as a man with the head of a jackal, and the statue was reportedly inscribed with a curse promising a terrible fate to anyone who entered.

Of course, Carter, Carnarvon, and their team ignored this as just ancient superstition, but soon, strange things began to happen.

Six weeks after entering the tomb, Lord Carnarvon died in his Cairo hotel room from an infected mosquito bite. George Gould, who had visited the tomb, died of a fever two months later. Arthur Mace, one of the excavation team, died within a few years under mysterious circumstances, as did Richard Bethel, Carter's secretary in Egypt, whose death was never explained. Howard Carter was diagnosed with cancer a few years later and lived for another 10 years before succumbing to the disease. Possibly the most mysterious event happened to Bruce Ingram, who visited the tomb and was given a paperweight as a gift by Carter – a mummified hand with a bracelet inscribed with another curse: "To whoever moves my body shall come fire, water, and pestilence." Shortly after receiving the gift, Ingram's house burned down. When it was rebuilt, it was again destroyed, this time by a flood.

Was it all an awful string of coincidences, or did the pharaoh's curse actually reach from beyond the grave? We will never know for sure, but just be careful next time you enter a pharaoh's tomb!

The Truth about the "Lunch on a Skyscraper" Photo

There are many photographs that people remember as icons of their times, encapsulating an event or a moment in history that will always be remembered. Photos of the Twin Towers on 9/11, or raising the Flag on Iwo Jima, or the photo of Che Guevara in his beret, or the execution of a prisoner on a Saigon street. One photo that is instantly recognizable is of a group of men, building workers, sitting on an iron girder atop a skyscraper under construction, high in the air over the streets of New York City.

Paying no attention to their perceived danger, the men are casually chatting while having lunch without any visible safety equipment or harnesses. This photo showed the world the toughness and resilience of the American spirit at the time of depression in the early 1930s.

Although it looked like an everyday occurrence for these men of steel, it was actually a publicity shot to promote the Rockefeller Center, which was the building under construction and was carefully staged, although the men were real workers. There were other photos taken at the same time showing men playing football on the beam and also men stretched out asleep on the beam, all hundreds of feet above street level.

But things are not always what they seem; the photo was taken from the side and appeared to show the iron girder hanging in the air suspended by steel cables, but in fact, the girder was actually about 6 feet above the concrete flooring, and it was just the angle of the shot that made it look like it was suspended above the street. If one of the men fell off, the worst that would happen would be that they might break an ankle, which is probably why they all look so casual just sitting and eating their lunch, 6 feet in the air.

Regardless of the facts, it has always symbolized the bravery of the American worker, although it has been copied and parodied many times. In one image, the workers are replaced by the cast of the Muppet Show. In another, the workers have been replaced with movie stars like Tom Cruise and Richard Gere. In yet another, the workers have been replaced by comic book heroes like Superman and the Hulk.

While this all may seem, at first glance, to be disrespectful, it is probably a case of imitation being the sincerest form of flattery.

The Cobra Effect

There is an old saying that the road to hell is paved with good intentions. An up-to-date version of this is the Law of Unintended Consequences, and it basically means that the more you try to do good in the world, the more likely the end result will be the opposite of what you intend.

The term "the Cobra Effect" came from an event in Delhi, India, during the time of British colonization.

At that time, the British governor became aware that there were venomous cobra snakes around the city and that a number of people had been bitten and had died from the bites. In an attempt to be seen as caring for the people of Delhi, the governor issued a reward to professional snake catchers to catch and kill cobras, thinking that this would reduce the snake population.

Initially, this worked well, and snake catchers were regularly catching the snakes around town. However, when people began to see the money being made by snake catchers, they started breeding cobras themselves in snake farms to sell to the snake catchers. The British authorities found out what was happening and canceled the bounty on dead snakes. As a result, all the people who had been breeding cobras realized they would not get any money for them, so they released them, bringing a huge rise in the snake population of Delhi – an unintended consequence.

A similar situation occurred in Hanoi during the time of French rule. In order to control the rat population, the French authorities promised a reward to anyone killing rats and bringing their tails as evidence. Like the cobras in Delhi, this started off well, but French policemen started to notice many rats around without tails – the local people were simply cutting tails off live rats and letting them return to breed so that more rats would be available and they could claim the reward for the tails!

The worst example happened in China in the 1950s. The country's leader, Chairman Mao, had heard many complaints that flocks of sparrows were damaging rice crops and spreading diseases, so he declared the sparrow to be a "capitalist enemy" to be eradicated, and rewards would be given to whoever handed in the deadest birds.

The people were enthusiastic, and there followed a wholesale slaughter of the sparrow population, leaving them almost extinct in China. However, it soon became apparent that in addition to rice plants, sparrows also ate many insects, including locusts. With few sparrows around, the number of insects suddenly increased and destroyed more of the rice crops than the sparrows ever did. This actually led to the Great Chinese Famine of 1960, when millions died of hunger. While Chairman Mao's intentions were for the best, his plan had serious unintended consequences.

“But I am the President”

We often think that some country’s politicians are a little crazy, and sometimes their actions confirm it. Paul Deschanel was President of France for just seven months in 1920 and became known for his eccentric behavior. He once read the same speech twice at a state dinner in the French city of Nice. President Deschanel was addressing the city leaders and business people, and the first half of his speech was received to great applause. He proceeded to read the same speech again, and the applause at the end of this was a little subdued and just out of politeness.

It turned out that, carried away at the moment, he had neglected to turn the page and did not realize that he was repeating his words. On another occasion, he was presented with a bouquet of flowers by some schoolgirls. Acting as if he was at a wedding, he threw the bouquet over his shoulder back at them, as in the bridal tradition. However, he was not really that crazy – he became the first President of France not to have any criminals executed during his term because he did not agree with the death penalty.

Toward the end of his term, he achieved the distinction of becoming the first head of state, in fact, the only one to fall from a moving train. It happened one night in May of 1920 on the Orient Express, traveling between two stations in France. Deschanel had given instructions not to be disturbed until 7 a.m. and had taken some sleeping medication. At some point in the night, perhaps due to the heat or maybe the effects of the medication, he got up for some fresh air. Opening the large window of the presidential suite on the train, he leaned out and promptly fell out of the window onto the tracks. No one noticed, and the train continued on, leaving him alone in the darkness. Luckily, the train had been moving fairly slowly, so he only sustained a few scratches. Wearing only his green silk pajamas, he stumbled along the train track until he reached a signal box and banged on the door. The signalman put his head out and said, "What do you want?" Deschanel shouted, "I am the president of France," to which the unimpressed signalman replied, "Yes, and I am Napoleon Bonaparte." Deschanel insisted, "But I am the president!" and eventually, the signalman called the chief of police, who identified Deschanel and escorted him to a local worker's cottage, where his staff were contacted to come and pick him up.

Shortly afterward, he was at a state meeting in a hotel by a lake. Without any warning, he walked out of the hotel and into the lake, fully clothed. Finally, his unstable mental state was recognized, and he was asked to resign. He was then sent to a psychiatric hospital for some time, and when he was released, he was reinstated to a political office – proving that you don't have to be crazy to work in politics, but it helps!

The Family of Oudh

There have been many attempts by con artists to pass themselves off as royalty in order to fool the gullible. Usually, it has been to get money by false pretenses, but in the case of the Royal Family of Oudh, it seems all they wanted was recognition.

It all started when an old lady appeared, seemingly from nowhere, on the platform at the train station in New Delhi, the capital of India. The lady announced that she was Wilyat, the Begum, or queen of Oudh. Oudh was a kingdom in India in the 1800s, which was conquered by the British and ceased to exist except for a few temples and shrines.

The old lady, Wilyat, said that all her palaces and properties had been stolen from her family, and she would stay at the station until they were restored to her. She settled into the waiting room with her family of two – Prince Ali Raza and Princess Sakina. They also brought along two Nepali servants, carpets, potted palms, a silver tea set, and two Great Danes. She insisted on being addressed as "Your Highness," and she would only answer questions if they were put in writing and handed to her on a silver tray.

The story spread throughout India, and most people in Lucknow, where the old kingdom of Oudh used to be located, believed her to be the rightful queen descended from the royal line of Oudh. The Indian government was very concerned about this because although most states in India were ruled by Hindus, the population of Lucknow was mainly Muslim, and the government did not want any trouble between the two factions.

Officials started trying to find somewhere suitable for the Begum and her family to live. They were offered several larger houses but refused each one as "too small." They wanted a palace. Finally, after living in the railway station for ten years, they were offered a "palace" by the prime minister, Indira Gandhi. It was, in fact, a 14th-century hunting lodge, almost hidden in a jungle area near Delhi known as the Malcha Mahal, the word mahal meaning palace.

Journalists from all over the world came to interview them, and for many years, they were a regular news item in the foreign press and in Lucknow. Eventually, in the 1990s, the Begum died, and her son and daughter lived for another 20 years in the dilapidated jungle palace.

After their deaths, the true story came to light. The last true ruler of Oudh, the Nawab, had gone into exile after the British conquest in the 1850s, and there was no remaining family.

The old lady who claimed to be the Begum was, in fact, Wilyat Butt, a housewife from Lucknow who had spent time in a mental institution from which she escaped and fled to Delhi with her family by train. She probably believed her own story that she was descended from royalty and convinced her son and daughter that they were prince and princess. She also managed to convince the Indian government and the whole city of Lucknow; perhaps because she was such a regal figure, everyone wanted to believe it was real.

Megastructure in Space

It has often been said that the massive Great Wall of China is so big that it can be seen from space. Maybe in the future, we will build something bigger that can be seen from so far away, but in the meantime, there is only the Great Wall.

However, astronomers have discovered something that looks like an alien structure that can be seen in space. The Kepler Space Telescope at NASA keeps a watch on distant parts of the universe and has found something strange around a star about a trillion lightyears away. A light year, as we all know, is how far we can travel in one year, moving at the speed of light, so a trillion of them would place it at the outer reaches of where we can possibly observe but certainly never travel to.

What the Kepler telescope has found is a star that regularly dims in brightness and seems to have something around it. Some scientists think this may prove the existence of what is called a Dyson Sphere. Freeman Dyson, a theoretical physicist, first came up with the theory that some stars seem to have a shell around them, like a megastructure built by alien inhabitants of distant galaxies. The purpose of this shell-like structure was to capture and contain the energy of the star, possibly to provide power to the aliens' home planet. The Kepler telescope identified what could be arrays of solar cells linked in space around the star, and as they rotated around the star, this regularly dimmed its brightness to our observation. Other scientists have dismissed these as just dust clouds, but their pattern seems to be very regular.

Part of the theory of the Dyson sphere is that as civilizations become more advanced, they will extract all the energy from their planet, then from their star, and then from the galaxy itself. While this all sounds like science fiction, it is a fact: the Dyson sphere would be one-way aliens would collect energy from a star.

One issue with all this is that, given the distance in lightyears that this sphere is from Earth, it means the light and images that we can see actually started traveling through space many thousands of years ago, in the time of the dinosaurs, in fact, and these alien civilizations may not even exist anymore if they did in the first place.

Bearing in mind that we will never be able to travel a trillion light years and the aliens are also in the same position, the truth of the Dyson sphere will never be known, which is one reason astrophysicists enjoy these theories, knowing they can never be proved or disproved. But it is a real possibility that the biggest structure that can be seen from space is not the Great Wall of China but an alien megastructure built to harness the solar power from a star.

The Teleporting Soldier

Incidences of time travel and teleportation have always been popular in science fiction stories, but sometimes, it seems that the truth is stranger than fiction.

In October 1593, the governor of the Philippines was assassinated at sea by Chinese pirates. A soldier, Gil Perez, was standing on guard overnight at the governor's palace in Manila in the Philippines in preparation for the ceremony to swear in a new president the following day. In those days, the islands of the Philippines were ruled by Spain, and Gil Perez was a Spanish soldier. During the night, Perez started to feel dizzy, and he leaned back against a wall and closed his eyes for a few seconds.

When he opened his eyes, he was suddenly not in the palace but in something like a town square surrounded by people. Astounded by this sudden change of scene, he thought he had sleepwalked into another part of Manila until he started to ask directions from the people around him, who told him he was actually in Mexico City, nearly 9,000 miles away from Manila. In a daze, he stumbled around, trying to make sense of this, and he was eventually picked up by local soldiers. They recognized that he had a military uniform but not one they had seen before, so they assumed he was some sort of army deserter and put him in prison to await a magistrate.

He tried explaining what happened and where he came from, but no one believed him. He told the officials about the assassination of the governor, but since, in those days, it took between 6 weeks and 3 months for ships to travel from Manila to Mexico, the news had not yet reached them, and they refused to believe Perez's story.

Perez was held in prison mainly because the authorities did not know what else to do with him until, eventually, a ship arrived from the Philippines with news of the governor's death. Some of the passengers even recognized his uniform as being a Manila palace guard. The officials realized that Perez had been telling the truth, so he was released and put on a ship back to Manila.

When he arrived home, he was again arrested for desertion, and the army had been looking for him ever since that night. However, the ship's captain explained the story of Perez in Mexico, and although it seemed completely outlandish, he was, in the end, believed and allowed to return to duty.

There is enough recorded historical evidence to support the story of Gil Perez in both Mexico City and Manila, one key fact being that rumors of the Philippine Governor's death circulated in Mexico City soon after it happened, although there was no way anyone could know until a ship came from Manila weeks later. This strange event has been blamed on astral travel, teleportation, and even alien abduction. What we do know is that historical records show it really happened, but of course, they don't say how.

A City Destroyed by Climate Change

The problem of climate change is the subject of concern and discussion all around the world, with many people believing we could soon be facing environmental disasters. Reports of hotter summers, colder winters, and all sorts of weather variations are always in the news as warning signs that things will get worse. All of this may be true today, but it is not the first time this has happened, and changes to climate caused the end of one of the world's greatest civilizations.

Angkor in Cambodia is the remains of a city that once housed over one million people and was built around 1,000 years ago. It was the capital of the ancient Khmer empire that reached across Asia. At one time, it was considered to be the biggest city in the world. At the center of the city was the Angkor Wat, a complex of temples and royal palaces covering over 500 acres, with towers over 200 feet high. The city was mysteriously abandoned after several hundred years, sometime in the 15th century, and the jungle took over.

Since its rediscovery in the mid-1800s, experts have been trying to understand what happened and to try to map out the scope of the city itself. What has always made it difficult was that although the Angkor Wat complex was constructed from stone, the surrounding city, the houses, shops, and other buildings were built from wood, so nothing has survived the ravages of time except the stone temples and palaces.

In 2012, a new technology was used to map the area, called LIDAR (Light Detection and Ranging). The LIDAR team flew a helicopter over the area and sent out billions of beams of light that passed through the jungle canopy and reflected off leaves, soil, and other features on the ground, giving a complete map of the terrain. Using LIDAR, they could see hundreds of hidden features that would have been dams, reservoirs, canals, and roads. These all showed how heavily the city depended on irrigation techniques and water storage in order to cultivate crops to feed the inhabitants of the city and provide fresh drinking water. It also measured the extent of the city at around 27 square miles, not including outlying villages.

They began to understand what had happened to the mighty city of Angkor. The economy of the city and the lives of the population depended on networks of water systems, storing and supplying water throughout the year from huge reservoirs, which were filled each year by the rains of the monsoon season, roughly from April to October. Historical records show that in the 14th and 15th centuries, the annual rainfall during the Monsoon season became unreliable and not as plentiful as it once was.

The theory is that this caused people to start to move out southwards toward the Tonle Sap Lake and down the river toward what is now Phnom Penh, where the Mekong River flows down through Vietnam. As water started to become scarce in the city, more people, including the royal family and priests, left the city until, eventually, there was nothing left except the jungle. By the time the monsoon rains returned in strength a hundred or so years later, it was too late, and so Angkor became a ghost city.

So, this is what can happen when the climate changes – not all at once, but gradually over time. The good news is that it is not always a man-made problem. The bad news is that it can still have disastrous consequences.

Men on the Moon – in 1835

It used to be the case that anything published in a newspaper was believed to be true, no matter how ridiculous, and many newspapers took advantage of this to carry out April Fools jokes on an unsuspecting public, a tradition carried on to this day. Lately, there has been much cynicism about "fake news," not only in print but also in online and other visual media, and we tend to be a little more questioning than in the past. However, in the mid-1800s, the newspaper was still seen as the source of truth, and anything published within its pages was treated with complete veracity. This led to one of the most elaborate hoaxes of those days – the Great Moon Hoax of 1835.

There were already claims that people lived on the moon. One astronomer, Franz Gruithuisen, claimed to be able to identify shades of color on the moon, indicating vegetation, solid structures that were possibly buildings, and straight lines that were roads. Another so-called expert, Thomas Dick, calculated that around 42 billion inhabitants lived on the moon. Both pseudo-scientists had strong followings, and their writings were accepted by many.

Then, the Sun, a New York newspaper, published a series of six articles about life on the moon in August of 1835. The articles were credited to Sir John Herschel, a well-respected English astronomer who was famous for having discovered the planet Uranus. The articles claimed that Herschel had built the biggest telescope in existence to map out the galaxy and, using this, had seen life on the moon in close-up. The Sun claimed that Herschel had seen vegetation and animals resembling small cattle, long-beaked birds, and playful goats. Strangest of all, he claimed to have spotted creatures that had the bodies of men but with wings like bats.

All the articles were accompanied by illustrations and drawings showing all the strange sights to be seen on the moon. The articles were widely believed, and some religious groups even made plans to travel to the moon for missionary purposes. Even rival papers like the New York Times were taken in, stating that this sort of life on the moon was "probable and possible." Other astronomers wanted to inspect this huge telescope, but in the last article, Herschel wrote that beams from the sun had been magnified by the telescope lens, and the observatory had caught fire, destroying everything, including the world's biggest telescope.

Eventually, the truth came out. The articles were written and created by a journalist called Richard Locke. He had recently started work at the Sun newspaper and realized that it had a very poor circulation compared to other New York newspapers, with around 8,000 readers each day. His motive was two-fold. He wanted to increase the sales of the paper through a sensational story and also poke fun at the other writers who had made outrageous claims about life on the moon, like Thomas Dick and Gruithuisen. Unfortunately, everyone believed his stories at first, and the circulation of the Sun increased dramatically and stayed high afterward, making it one of New York's major daily papers.

As for the real John Herschel, he was initially amused by having his name tied in with the hoax, but he soon became annoyed by people asking him questions about life on the moon, so he asked the Sun to print a full retraction stating the whole story was a hoax. The editor of the Sun agreed in order to keep Herschel quiet, but the retraction was never printed, and after a while, a new story came along, and the public forgot all about it. So, was this an early example of fake news?

The Secrets of Stonehenge

Large-scale construction is not so hard these days, with highly qualified engineers and designers and an enormous variety of equipment to make every job simple. Thousands of years ago, things were quite different, though. There were no universities offering courses in engineering and architecture and no equipment except for roughly constructed tools made from rope and wood. However, the ancient people managed to construct some amazing monuments, and many are still a mystery in terms of how they were made and what they were made for.

One of these is Stonehenge, a prehistoric monument in Wiltshire, England, which dates back to 3100 BC, around 5,000 years ago. It consists of a ring of large upright rectangular stones, all connected at the top with stones like lintels over a doorway. Inside this ring is a ring of smaller stones. The outer ring of stones is sarsen stone, a rock-like material that was quarried and transported to Stonehenge from Marlborough, about 20 miles away. The average weight of these sarsen stones is 25 tons.

The inner ring of stones are bluestones, so called because they appear blue when wet or split. The bluestones were brought from west Wales, about 175 miles away, and weigh on average 10 tons. So, the first question we have is, how did these people with primitive tools (before the invention of the wheel) transport these enormous heavy stones so far? The theory is that the stones were laid on huge wooden sledges and dragged across the country, a process that would take many weeks to move just one stone.

The next problem would be shaping the stones. In their natural state, the stones would just be huge boulders and had to be cut into shape using primitive hammer stones. These were just round rocks that would be used to chip away at the boulders to square off the edges. The most amazing part was how the top stones were fixed onto the standing stones. They were not just laid on top; each top stone had two concave holes shaped into it, and the standing stones had two convex shapes protruding from the top so they could be fitted together. The top lintel stones also fitted with each other with joints that today are only seen in cabinet-making. The whole thing was a masterpiece of planning and engineering, but the third question is, why? What made these early Britons go to all this trouble?

The answer is that no one really knows, but there are many theories. Surrounding Stonehenge are many ancient burial mounds, and many human remains have been excavated around the stones, leading some people to think the whole site was a temple for druids to carry out burial rites or human sacrifices. Another theory is that it was built to keep track of the passing year since it is aligned with the summer and winter solstice, and the number of stones correlates to the months and weeks of the ancient Egyptian calendar – although no one suggests that it was built by the same people who built the pyramids. The only people who knew what it was for were the people who constructed it, and unfortunately, they had no written language to record their reasons or methods, so we will never know the real secrets of Stonehenge.

We are all Martians

Mars is our nearest planet and has always been the subject of science fiction stories. It is known, of course, that there is no life on Mars, and various unmanned expeditions have mapped the planet and brought back samples of the rocks and dust. But what about the idea from the latest theories that millions of years ago, there was some form of life on Mars? Not only that, but it somehow traveled to Earth and became the early life forms from which all living creatures descended? What if we were all Martians? This might sound like a crazy idea straight out of a science fiction novel, but in fact, many scientists believe this is exactly the case.

One expedition first made the intriguing discovery that although it is now a dry planet, at one time in its history, there was actually water on Mars. This has been confirmed by other expeditions, and this may have supported life probably in the form of bacteria and microbes. A key point, however, is that traces of the element molybdenum have also been found, and this is normally only found where there is oxygen, leading scientists to believe that Mars once had an atmosphere. Many other trace elements have been discovered on Mars that would have supported and developed life.

What is exciting about the discovery of molybdenum is that it is crucial in evolving life forms. Heat, light, and water may be needed to grow a life form from a microbe into an organism, but molybdenum is one of the main elements needed to bind all the ingredients together in the first place. It is known that originally, the Earth was covered completely by water with no land, and there was no oxygen, so any molybdenum on Earth had to have come from Mars. As the planets evolved, many asteroids, lumps of rock, were constantly flying around, and it is believed that asteroids from Mars struck the Earth many times millions of years ago, not only bringing the elements needed for life but possibly microbes that were the start of life itself. So unbelievable as it may be, it seems that life started not on Earth but on Mars and piggy-backed on asteroids to get here, and those microbes and bacteria became cells and organisms and, over millions of years, evolved into all the life on our planet.

So, the answer to the question is, yes, we are all Martians!

The Green Children of Woolpit

There are many strange stories passed down to us through history that came about by people in early times and the Middle Ages just not being able to understand or comprehend an unusual or completely natural event, leading to myths about giants, fairies, and demons. Occasionally, the story itself is a bit strange, and even today, it is difficult to unravel the mystery. This is the case of a well-documented occurrence that took place in the Village of Woolpit in Suffolk, England, sometime in the late 12th century, about 1180 AD.

The villagers were startled when two children, a boy, and a girl, suddenly appeared next to a wolf pit, a big pit used as a trap for wolves that roamed the land in those days, and after which the village was named. Not only did the sudden appearance of the children alarm the villagers, but also that they wore unusual clothes, they spoke in a strange language, and their skin was green. They were taken to the home of the local lord, Richard de Calne, who took them in and cared for them.

At first, they would not eat any food given to them, but then they found some green beans in the garden and ate them raw. De Calne incorporated these into their diet, and gradually, the two children started to eat other food. After a time, the children's green skin faded to a more normal color, and they began to learn English.

At that point, De Calne decided that the children should be baptized to make sure they were Christians, so he took them to the local church for the baptismal ceremony. However, shortly after being baptized, the boy became ill and died. The girl stayed healthy, and when she learned to speak English, she told a strange story. She said she and her brother had been herding cattle in a land far away where everything was green; it was always twilight, and the sun never shone. They had gone into a cave to rest, and when they came out, they were in a different place, by the wolf pit, and that was all they knew.

The girl worked as a servant for De Calne for many years before marrying a local man and settling down. History does not record what happened to her or if she had any children, green or otherwise.

Theories range from alien abduction, teleportation, or the children stepping out of a parallel universe, but no reasonable explanation was ever found for their sudden arrival. However, it is commonly thought that they had wandered from a Flemish settlement some distance away and that their green skin was caused by chlorosis, a symptom of dietary deficiency that gives the skin a green tinge and is solved by a better diet.

As always, the truth is out there, but given the passing of so many centuries, we will never be sure exactly what happened.

City of Ghosts

There have been many brutal dictators throughout history, men who wanted to rule the world or just rule their own people with an iron fist. In some cases, a political leader has a strange idea and decides to make the whole country follow it, and this is what happened in Cambodia in 1975.

Saloth Sar, better known to the world as Pol Pot, was educated at a University in France in the early 1950s, at a time when France was the colonial power in Southeast Asia, governing Vietnam, Laos, and Cambodia. Despite his advantages, he hated French rule and began to study communist theory, and when he returned to Cambodia in the 1960s after the French had left, he led the Cambodian communist party. The ordinary people of Cambodia are known as Khmer, and the communists were called the Red Khmer or Khmer Rouge.

Cambodia suffered greatly during the 1960s and early 1970s because its neighbor, Vietnam, was at war with America, and the Americans often carried out bombing raids on parts of Cambodia that they thought sheltered Vietnamese troops. In 1975, the war finally finished, and the Americans left. Pol Pot decided that Cambodia, then a monarchy with a royal family, would be communist, and he led an army against the royal government in a civil war.

Pol Pot's forces were successful, and the monarchy was overthrown. Pol Pot installed himself as prime minister, and then it became apparent that he had strange ideas to turn the country around. He decided that all industry would stop and only farming would be allowed.

He declared that 1975 was Year Zero, when the country would begin again as an agrarian economy, with the whole population working in the fields to produce rice and other crops. He wanted everyone to only focus on this, and he declared education, administration, science, medicine, and everything that was not related to farming should stop immediately. He also wanted to dismantle the family unit so that men, women, and children would only be loyal to the communist party and not to their families.

To carry out his strange ideas, he ordered his soldiers to go into every town and city and force people to leave their homes and work in the fertile Northeast areas of the country on communal farms. The most spectacular case was in the capital city of Phnom Penh. This was a city of two million people, and over the course of three days, Pol Pot's soldiers forced every single inhabitant out of their homes and made them start walking on the road to the Northeast, around Siem Reap, a distance of around 200 miles. The entire city was emptied, all the houses, the hospitals, even the jails, until there was not one living person left in the city, like a ghost city.

Of course, Pol Pot's grand ideas did not last. A new government with more democratic ideas was formed, and with the help of Vietnamese troops, the Khmer Rouge was pushed out. People gradually returned to the towns and cities, and Phnom Penh once again became a bustling capital city, but even today, it is still called the City of Ghosts.

The Strangest Monuments

Most towns have something that makes them a little different. A big fountain, the tallest buildings, and some different features that people recognize. Some towns, however, are known for their odd choice of monument. A great example of this is a town in Oregon, USA, called Fairview. Fairview has the world's biggest fork. A 37-foot, 2.5-ton sculpture of a fork has been installed at a food plaza, and the town is currently waiting to see if it will be a world record in the Guinness Book of Records.

New Zealand hosts some strange monuments. The town of Ohakune is in the center of a vegetable-growing region, and visitors to the town are welcomed by the sight of a 30-foot carrot on the main road into town. Another small town, Paeroa, is famous for its sparkling spring waters, which for decades have been bottled with lemon juice and sold as Lemon & Paeroa, known in NZ as L&P. In the center of the town sits a huge bottle of L&P, nearly 22 feet high.

In Paris, the home of the Eiffel Tower and the Louvre, there is also a little-known monument, a 35-foot-high bronze sculpture of an artist's thumb. It is supposed to be a symbol of good luck, "thumbs up," and is in the business district where they probably need all the luck they can get.

In Taiwan, in the town of Budai, there is a shoe – not just a shoe, a lady's shoe made of blue glass, and it stands nearly 60 feet tall. It was originally designed as a church but was never used, now, it is just an odd monument.

Australia is often called "down under," so it is no surprise that their strangest monument is an upside-down statue. The whole statue of a man, Charles Latrobe, including the plinth, is turned upside down with Mr. Latrobe's head half buried in the grass. Latrobe was the governor of Victoria in Australia, and the university is named after him. The idea is that when you go to university, you should look at everything from a different point of view.

Balls of twine are a common monument, and they can be quite competitive. In Darwin, Minnesota, USA, a man called Johnson rolled a ball of twine four hours a day for 29 years. There was probably not much else to do in Darwin, a town of 350 inhabitants. Anyway, he ended up with a ball of twine 12-foot wide, and it sits next to the town's water tower. Frank Stoeber in Cawker City, Kansas, tried to beat the record but could only manage a ball with a width of 11 feet. Still, he used 1.6 million feet of twine, which is very impressive.

There are many odd monuments around the world, and it is always a wonder what inspires folk to want to have something like the biggest fork in their town. But they do, and that is what makes the world such an interesting place.

The Big Grey Man of Macdhui

You will have heard about the Yeti in the Himalayan mountains and the Bigfoot creature supposed to roam the woods of North America, but you may not have heard of the Big Grey Man of Macdhui in Scotland.

Ben Macdhui is a mountain in Scotland, and at nearly 4,500 feet, it is the second-highest peak in the country. It is known locally as the Haunted Mountain thanks to local legends about an unnatural Big Grey Man who is said to haunt the mountain. It first came to be known when John Collie, a respected mountaineer and professor at London University, spoke about an experience he had when climbing Ben Macdhui in 1891.

As he walked down the mountain through a patch of mist, he heard footsteps matching his own, crunching on the gravel track. When he stopped, the footsteps stopped, and when he started walking again, the footsteps started again. Looking around, he could see nothing through the fog, but he suddenly felt scared and moved off the mountain as fast as he could.

Several other people, over the years, also had the same experience but did not see anything. Then, two brothers who were hiking in the mountains came back with a strange story.

One of the brothers was Dr A.M. Kellas, a well-known mountaineer who would not make up a story like that. The brothers said that as they stopped for a rest, out of the mist came a terrifying figure, a tall thin grey man, about 10 feet tall. The brothers panicked and raced down the mountain, convinced the grey man was chasing them. Many years later, there was another sighting. A climber named Sydney Scroggie was resting at a spot overlooking a lake when he saw a strange tall figure walking on the other side of the lake.

There have been plenty of sightings, and in one incident, a man tried to shoot the grey man. Alexander Tewnion was walking along a mountain pass when he heard something rushing toward him. He looked around to see a ghostly shape, a tall grey figure, running straight at him. Tewnion drew a pistol and fired three shots, and the figure disappeared, but there was no evidence of blood or any sign of a creature.

Despite the many sightings, no one has ever got close enough to identify the creature, and that is quite understandable. It is one of those unknown monsters that live in strange places or in the imagination. In fact, most theories tend to suggest the sightings were probably hallucinations or imagination brought on by fatigue or loneliness. Walking through a high mountain pass alone in swirling mist, anyone could imagine something was there. Regardless, the truth may one day be known, and the secret of the Big Grey Man is revealed.

The Man With a Third Eye

In the 1950s, before the obsession with Eastern mysticism of the 1960s, ordinary folk in the Western world knew very little about Buddhism and even less about Tibet, a country high in the mountains of the Himalayas, where the Yeti was said to walk, and where the movie Shangri-La was set. A man called Tuesday Lobsang Rampa, usually known as T. Lobsang Rampa, became well known through his writings about Buddhism, mainly his book The Third Eye, about his childhood and early years. He claimed to have been born in Tibet to a wealthy family, and at age seven, he was sent to a monastery to become a monk.

At the monastery, high on the mountain peaks in Tibet, he studied medicine, astrology, telepathy, hypnotism, and the theory of reincarnation. He also said that he underwent a painful operation to open up a third eye in the middle of his forehead, during which a piece of silver was implanted in his forehead, which gave him amazing psychic powers.

After many years he left the monastery and roamed the land, and during WW2, he was captured by Japanese soldiers and interned in a prison camp for most of the war. Most of the prisoners there were British soldiers, and from them, he learned to speak, read, and write English. After being released from the camp, he traveled to England, where he set up a Buddhist school, passing on his knowledge, and he wrote several books, including The Third Eye. In the book, he claims to have met a Yeti and to have come across his own mummified body from a previous life. He also said that in Tibet, people were named after the day of the week on which they were born, hence his name, Tuesday.

Eventually, his writings were studied by a renowned scholar of Tibetan Buddhism, Heinrich Harrer, who disproved many of the stories in the book, especially the one about the third eye. Harrer said that in Tibetan mythology, the third eye is opened by peaceful meditation, not by a painful operation. Harrer was angry and believed Rampa to be a fraud, so he hired a private detective to investigate. Then the truth came out. Rampa was, in fact, Cyril Hoskins, born in Devon, England, the son of a plumber. He had worked in Devon most of his life and had never traveled outside England. He had always been fascinated by the occult and the mysterious, and one day, he just shaved his head and changed his name. For a while, he fooled the public into believing he was a mystical Tibetan monk named Lobsang Rampa.

However, when he was finally tracked down and confronted with his true identity, he admitted he was born Cyril Hoskins but that his soul had been taken over in the process of reincarnation by an ancient Buddhist monk and that everything in the book was true. Despite being proven to be a phony, many people still believed his story, and his books still sold. Hoskins died in 1981, still insisting he was actually T. Lobsang Rampa in another body, and who knows, maybe he was.

Grow Taller and Live Longer in Space

Many of us are sometimes unhappy with parts of our bodies – people often want to change the shape of their nose or chin, remove wrinkles, and surgically reduce fat, not to mention the various alterations some women like to make to their bodies. One thing that we always believed can never be altered is our height. If a person feels they are a bit short and would like to be taller, there is nothing they can do about it.

Except maybe there is: NASA scientists have found that an astronaut who spends some time in space actually grows taller. This is due to the effect of zero gravity, like in a space capsule or on the international space station. On Earth, the force of gravity keeps us on the ground by pulling us down, and the atmosphere also exerts pressure on us as we move around. In a zero-gravity situation, the force and pressure is gone, allowing our spine to decompress and stretch, with the result that astronauts who have spent a while in zero gravity return to Earth a couple of inches taller. In one case, a Japanese astronaut, Norishge Kanai, claimed that after three weeks in space, he had grown three inches in height. There is bad news, however – on return to Earth, the forces of gravity and atmospheric pressure soon start to compress the spine again, and the height returns to what it was before.

Another amazing change to bodies in space is that astronauts can live longer. This was found when studying identical twins – one in space, one in a controlled situation on Earth. What scientists found was that in space, parts of our DNA that control aging are altered. Basically, we have something called telomeres that control how many times our cells renew themselves, and over time these telomeres grow shorter as we age. In space, however, these telomeres were found to actually grow longer, meaning we would age more slowly. However, once back on Earth, the process reverses.

So, the moral is to be taller and live longer, you have to live in outer space – permanently!

The Mothman

Every culture seems to have its strange monster that sometimes appears but is never really identified – the Yeti, Bigfoot, the Loch Ness monster, and many others like the Mothman, which was first seen in West Virginia, USA, in the 1960s. The first reported sighting was by five men who were digging a grave when they saw a shadowy, man-sized figure flying over their heads. Three days later, a young couple claimed they were chased in their car by a huge flying creature with a 10-foot wingspan. Many other sightings were reported, usually at night, of a large man-sized bird with glowing red eyes. These all happened near the small town of Point Pleasant, where there was an old military munitions dump and a disused nuclear facility. Many locals believed that the Mothman was a result of nuclear testing and that experiments were still being carried out in secret at the government facility.

After a while, there were sightings in different parts of the country, such as Chicago, where at least 55 people claim to have seen a man-sized bird with glowing eyes flying above them. Rumors spread of similar sightings in other countries, usually linked to nuclear facilities. For example, the Mothman was seen near Chernobyl, the scene of major radiation leakage.

These days, the town of Point Pleasant, where the Mothman was first seen, holds a Mothman festival every year with live music, carnival rides, food stalls, and trips to places where the Mothman had been spotted. The Mothman story has also been made into a movie and was the subject of a popular book.

There have been many possible explanations for the Mothman. Conspiracy theorists insist that it was the result of secret government nuclear experiments, radiation leaking from a nuclear power plant, or maybe secret attempts by the military to create a super-soldier who could fly into battle. Other explanations are more mundane, perhaps a bit more realistic. Scientific observers think it could be linked to the annual migration of Sandhill cranes, a bird with a large wingspan and red markings around its eyes. Others suggest it could be a barn owl, which has a larger wingspan than we think and has red reflective eyes at night. Regarding sightings in other places, that is put down to hallucinations caused by mass hysteria or wishful thinking. People hearing stories about the Mothman, seeing a large bird at night, then making a wrong connection.

Whatever it really was, so far, no one has been able to say for definite, and like the other mythical monsters, it makes a good "unknown" tale, but just maybe we may one day know the truth about the Mothman.

The Crystal Skull of Doom

The images we are used to seeing from Ancient South American civilizations like Aztecs and Mayans usually show strangely carved figures of their Gods, odd-looking sculptures that do not look human and are representative of their ideas rather than true-to-life images. However, some artifacts have been discovered that bear a really uncanny resemblance to the real thing, and they are the Crystal Skulls.

These are accurate copies of human skulls, and there are only about 12 in the world that have been found. Some are made from clear crystal, others from colored quartz crystal, and they are believed to originate from Mexico and Central America. Many people believe they were carved up to ten thousand years ago by an ancient civilization. Some people even think because they are unlike anything else produced by indigenous Aztecs or Mayans, that they may be from the lost city of Atlantis or even from aliens who visited the Aztecs before the Spanish arrived. Legends about the skulls talk about their supernatural powers, like claims of healing and psychic powers among people who have had contact with the skulls.

One particular school of thought that actually has a large following is that the skulls are a form of advanced computer recording energy and vibrations around them and that they contain the history of the planet within them if we could just work out how to get it. To be fair, most scientists are skeptical about that idea.

The most well-known of these skulls is called the Mitchell-Hedges skull. In 1924, a British explorer, Frederick Mitchell-Hedges, led an expedition to an ancient city deep in the jungles of Belize, where inside a Mayan pyramid, he found a skull made from a single piece of clear quartz crystal with a moveable jaw. Mitchell-Hedges claimed it was a relic from the Mayan era, and he called it “the Skull of Doom” because a number of people who were associated with it became ill, and some died – although obviously not Mr. Mitchell-Hedges. He also said he had heard of a native Indian philosophy that when all the crystal skulls were reunited together, they would reveal secrets that humankind would need to survive.

Another crystal skull was found by a family of Mayan descent in Guatemala in 1909. It was a strange shape unlike all the others, and in 1999, it came into the possession of a Dutch spiritualist who said it was the skull of an alien visitor who came from a planet over 400 light years away. The lady, Mrs. Joky van Dieten, travels the world with it, claiming it has mysterious healing powers, and she uses it to cure people.

Scientists who have examined the skulls say that the crystal quartz is unlike anything that can be found in the Central American region and that the sort of tools needed to carve them would not have existed in the ages before the landing of Columbus. This adds to the mystery for some people; others see it as an explanation that they were made more recently. Whatever the explanation, they are beautifully made artifacts, and whether from an ancient civilization or from outer space, they will always be objects of wonder.

Kuldhara: the Ghost Village

The village of Kuldhara in Rajasthan, India, has existed since early times and was a prosperous village inhabited mainly by people of the Brahmin caste, one of the high levels in the Hindu caste system. For centuries, the villagers lived peacefully until suddenly, over one night, the village was abandoned – every single person left and never returned.

There are many stories about the abandonment of Kuldhara. The story most often told, which has become a local legend, is that the Minister of State, Salim Singh, fell in love with the daughter of the village chief and wanted to marry her. The village chief refused because he thought Salim Singh was not a good man. Salim Singh insisted that he would marry the girl, and if the village chief denied him, he would attack the village with his soldiers and kill everyone. The village council met to discuss this and decided they would leave the village and start again, far away. They did this, but before leaving, they laid a curse on the village, saying that no one would ever live there in peace again. Subsequently, anyone who tried to settle there was chased out by the evil spirits of the curse.

Another more likely explanation is that Salim Singh, whom history records as a cruel and greedy State Minister, raised the taxes on the village to the point where it became too difficult to live under such a regime, so all the villagers left. Other more natural explanations have been suggested, including a lack of water supply due to many years of drought or even an Earthquake. Or maybe the evil spirits inhabited the place first and scared all the villagers away.

Kuldhara is today well-known as a ghost village, and many visitors report feeling the eerie presence of the long-departed villagers.

At one point, a team for a Paranormal Society in New Delhi decided to spend the night there. They claim that their ghost-detection equipment registered unusual activity, and they all felt someone touching their shoulders and calling out their names. Apart from them, no one else has ever been able to spend a night in the abandoned village.

In 2010, the governor of Rajasthan decided to develop it as a tourist destination, with accommodation not in the village but in nearby places. Visitors come from all over India, and even foreign tourists include it in their itinerary, even though it is known as one of the most haunted places in India.

The Discovery of the Blobs

How much do you really know about your planet? It seems that these days, people know more about outer space than they know about the Earth itself. For example, what do you know about the Blobs?

The ground we stand on, which we call the Earth, is the outer crust of the planet. Under this, about 30 to 50 kilometers under the Earth's surface, is a thick layer of silicone rock called the mantle, which makes up most of the planet's mass and is around 3,000 kilometers deep. Inside this is the core, a big ball of molten rock and minerals.

Just where the mantle meets the core are some strange oddities – enormous blobs of hot rock, about the size of continents, jutting out in every direction. Geologists do not know a lot about these and call them various names like "thermo-chemical piles" and "large velocity provinces," but usually, they are just known as "the blobs."

Two of the biggest blobs sit deep below the Pacific Ocean and are so big that if they were on the Earth's surface, they would stand about 100 times higher than Mount Everest.

Because of the depth at which the blobs live, geologists can only calculate their size and shape by looking at sound waves that travel through them. These sound waves are generated by earthquakes and the movements of plates on the Earth. The hot, dense blobs can slow down the sound waves, making it possible for geologists to estimate their size. The slowest and hottest ones are called "ultra-low velocity zones" (ULVZ), and the biggest ones of these are found under the Earth's crust in volcanic regions like Hawaii and other Pacific islands.

The theory is that seismic earthquake activity deep within the Earth pushes up the blobs, which are made of hot molten rock, and create hot spots on the Earth's surface, which is how volcanoes are formed.

That is just one theory, but the fact remains that even our best scientists still know less about our own planet than they know about the stars.

The Mystery of the Nazca Lines

Recent history is full of tales of aliens from outer space abducting people and flying their UFOs around the world. Mostly, there are practical explanations for all of these, although there are a few instances that we cannot explain rationally. One of the most intriguing examples of other-worldly occurrences is the Nazca Lines in Peru.

These were geometric lines carved into the desert in Peru, South America, near the town of Nazca. It is believed that they were made around 2,000 years ago but were only identified in the early 20th century after the invention of the airplane because they are almost impossible to see at ground level. They were first seen in 1924 by a commercial airline pilot flying over the Peruvian desert in the 1930s.

There are straight lines, called geoglyphs, which run for up to 30 miles, and there are around 800 of them in the desert. There are also 300 abstract geometric designs up to 1,200 feet long, and there are 70 other designs called biomorphs that represent plants and animals. Some of the biomorphs show spiders, monkeys, and hummingbirds, and all the designs cover a huge area of around 750 square kilometers.

There are many theories explaining the Nazca lines, apart from the "made by aliens" theory. Some archaeologists believe they have a ritual significance, tied into the religion of the original Nazca people who lived in the area and are connected to the worship of the gods who controlled the rains and water in general, a precious resource in a desert country.

Another explanation is that they have an astronomical purpose, like a giant calendar that measures the passage of the year through the movement of stars. Some of the longest lines align with the solstices, and some align with the rising and setting of the sun at certain times of the year.

The biggest question is, what inspired the native people of ancient Peru to make lines and designs that could only be seen from the air by someone or something flying above them? It would have been impossible for these early line-builders to know what they looked like, so how and why did they do it? Was it an attempt to communicate with extra-terrestrial life, and did those native people know more about aliens than we do now?

Is that Moby Dick or Mocha Dick?

We have all heard of Moby Dick, and although not everyone has read the book by Herman Melville or even seen one of the movies made about it, we all know it is about a great white whale that was hunted by a boatload of whalers armed with harpoons and their crazy captain, Captain Ahab. At the end of the story, the whale manages to sink the whaler's ship, and all the whalers are lost at sea except the one who narrates the story in the book.

What many people do not know is that the great white whale actually existed. The Moby Dick story was inspired by a giant albino whale that was well known to whalers in the early 1800s, a male sperm whale that lived in the Pacific Ocean and was usually seen in the waters near Mocha Island off the coast of Chile. This whale came to be known as Mocha Dick, and just like his fictional counterpart Mocha Dick survived many battles with whalers.

The whale was very large and powerful and capable of wrecking small boats with a thrash of his tail. The explorer Jeremiah Reynolds had first-hand experience of this mighty whale and described it as "an old bull whale of prodigious size and strength, white as wool, with a head covered in barnacles." Whaling at that time was the chief pastime and employment of sailors in Nantucket in North America, and they would sail all around South America through the Pacific Ocean hunting for whales, so the story of Mocha Dick was told in many a Nantucket tavern where sailors would meet, which is no doubt where Herman Melville heard the legend of the great white whale.

Many ships attempted to hunt Mocha Dick, and initially, the whale seemed quite docile, swimming alongside the whaling ships. But when attacked, Mocha Dick reacted with ferocious cunning, and he was feared by harpooners. The whale would sound a booming noise and then breach, throwing almost his whole body completely out of the water, coming down with a tremendous crash that could sink a small boat.

Sadly, Mocha Dick was killed by whalers in 1838. His body was 70 feet long and yielded 100 barrels of whale oil, along with a quantity of ambergris, a substance used in perfume manufacture, which at that time was more valuable than gold. He was also found to have more than 20 harpoons in his body, souvenirs of previous encounters with whalers. Nowadays, the sperm whale is listed as an endangered species, and hunting them is not allowed, so they get to live out their lives in peace, but that happened too late for Mocha Dick.

Radio Signals from Deep Space

Fundamentally, not many people really believe in aliens in outer space. Maybe we are too skeptical, or because we know that all of the stars and planets we can possibly see are incapable of supporting life, and those we can't see are so far away it would take many thousands of years for anyone to reach us here. However, that does not mean we give up on the idea, and there is an official institute known as SETI, the Search for Extra-terrestrial Intelligence, which monitors radio signals from outer space. Most of these signals come from the radiation produced by stars and galaxies and are in random patterns that have no meaning, just space background noise.

There are also things called Fast Radio Bursts (FRBs) that last just a couple of seconds and are thought to be from an exploding star somewhere in the universe. It is thought that FRBs have been happening for millions of years, but they only started to be recognized in 2007 as the equipment used became more sophisticated.

But sometimes, there is something that seems a bit more than just a random signal. Apparently, scientists and astronomers have been picking up a regular FRB that seems to be a radio signal sent to Earth every 16 days, and this has been happening for nearly two years. It is believed to come from a galaxy about 500 million light-years away, so it is currently impossible to know exactly where it originates, whether from a star or a planet and why it is being sent.

What actually happens is that for four days in a row, there are FRBs every hour, then it stops, and for 12 days, there is silence. Then it starts again, for four days, sending out a burst every hour, then it stops again for 12 days. This pattern has been repeated consistently for nearly two years, and to say it is baffling scientists is an understatement.

One possible theory is that the FRB comes from a spinning star that throws out a radio pulse as it revolves, and it then orbits around a bigger star, which stops the FRB from being sent until it has finished a 12-day orbit. Of course, there is another theory that an advanced alien civilization is sending out a deliberate pattern through the universe to see if there is anybody out there - however, given that traveling at the speed of light for 500 million years is just not possible, we may never know the truth, until our scientists get even better equipment and someone invents warp speed travel!

Michelangelo the Forger

Everyone has heard of the famous Italian sculptor and painter Michelangelo. He lived in 13th-century Rome and made some of the greatest art masterpieces in the history of the world, including his wonderful painting on the ceiling of the Sistine Chapel in the Vatican. But not many people know that he started out in his career as a forger. Initially, he was not always celebrated as a great artist, and in fact, in his early years when he was starting out, he struggled to make a living.

As a teenager, he worked with a well-known artist, Lorenzo de Medici, and gained a reputation for talent and ability far beyond his age and experience. But despite his obvious potential, he was seen as just another starving artist trying to sell his work. This was a difficult time for artists since most wealthy collectors were more interested in buying classic pieces from previous Roman and Greek times rather than buying what was considered "modern" artworks.

So, to make some money, Michelangelo hatched a devious plan. He created a beautiful sculpture of a sleeping cupid, which he then treated with acid to make it look like an old, weather-stained sculpture. He then buried it in the garden of a friend, who dug it up again and pretended to have discovered an ancient artwork centuries old.

It was sold to an art dealer, who later sold it to a Cardinal, Riario di San Giorgio. Cardinals in those days were generally wealthy and powerful members of the church. Unfortunately, the cardinal discovered it was a fake and sent it back to the dealer, demanding his money back. Although he was very angry at the fraud, the cardinal recognized that it was still a good sculpture, and he invited Michelangelo to meet with him and to talk about creating some genuine works of art for him. Through this, Michelangelo developed a strong relationship with the officials of the church in Rome, who would eventually give him some of his most celebrated art commissions.

This was the start of Michelangelo's career, and although his talent was bound to have been recognized sooner or later, it was his work as a forger that gave him a great impetus on his journey to become one of history's greatest artists.

As for the fake sculpture, it passed through many hands over time, and in the 1600s, it was bought by an English merchant trader, who brought it back to London and presented it to the king, Charles I. Sadly, it was destroyed in the Great Fire of London in 1666 when Whitehall Palace, where it was stored, burned down. Although it was a fake copy of an ancient statue, it would still be priceless today as one of Michelangelo's early works.

The Longest War with No Casualties

It sounds very strange to hear about a war where no one got hurt, but that is exactly what happened. It all started during a civil war in England between those who supported King Charles, the Royalists, and those who supported Oliver Cromwell, the Parliamentarians. Cromwell wanted England to be ruled by a democratic parliament rather than by the king and his courtiers, and there was a bitter war between 1642 and 1651.

Cromwell's forces succeeded in pushing the Royalists all the way off the mainland of Cornwall in the Southwest of England, and they took refuge in a group of islands off the Cornish coast, the Scilly Isles.

To get supplies to survive, the Royalists turned to piracy and attacked a number of merchant ships from the Netherlands, who had an alliance with the Parliamentarians. The Dutch navy then sent an Admiral with a fleet of warships to the Royalist fleet on Scilly to demand compensation. The Royalists refused, and the Dutch Admiral declared war on them. Since the rest of England was already in the hands of Cromwell's forces, war was only declared on the Scilly Isles. Faced with this threat, and also with the threat of attack from the Parliamentarian ships, the Royalists surrendered without a single shot being fired, and the Dutch ships sailed away, their honor satisfied. However, as it turned out, no peace treaty was ever signed, so technically, the Scillies and Holland were still at war.

This state continued until 1986 when a local Scilly historian, Roy Duncan, came across some old records that showed the conflict was still officially unresolved. Mr. Duncan then wrote to the Dutch Ambassador in London, who instructed his staff to search their records, and it was discovered that Mr. Duncan was correct – Holland and the Scillies were still at war.

After some negotiation, the Dutch Ambassador traveled to the Scillies in April 1986, and there signed an official peace treaty with the local town council, bringing an end after 335 years to what was the longest war in history, the only war with no battles and not a single casualty.

The Amazing Telescope

Usually, great discoveries are made by men of science, and many people throughout history have studied the heavens and tried to understand our universe. Sometimes, it is more simple people who make the discoveries. This certainly was the case with John Bradbury, a chiropodist from England who, in the 1950s, invented a new type of telescope that had 15 lenses. His theory was that the more lenses you have in a telescope, the farther you can see into space, even to the edge of the universe.

He claimed to have seen it already and that it showed him the whole universe was like a square box made of metal. He also said his telescope allowed him to study the Earth in more detail than ever seen before, and he could confirm that the Earth's surface was flat on the top like a table and round underneath so that the whole planet was like a solid ball cut in half.

He also made incredible discoveries about the moon. He said he saw it was a thin shell made of carbon one or two inches thick and actually a convex shape like a dented soccer ball. It traveled around the Earth, and every day, it accumulated larger amounts of plasticine from somewhere he did not know where. The plasticine was phosphorescent, which accounted for the moon shining at night.

The moon collected more and more plasticine as the month went on until it was completely covered, and this was a full moon. Because the weight of all this was too much, it started to fall off, accounting for the various phases of the moon, until there was none left, and the moon could not be seen. One night in 1953, he made his most bizarre discovery; Bradbury claimed to be able to see a giant finger coming out of the moon itself.

Like with any strange theories, there were some people who believed him, but mostly everyone was skeptical. When journalists asked to see the telescope, he always refused and said it was such a delicate mechanism only he could handle it. No one else was able to confirm any of his weird discoveries since no one else had a telescope like his.

Other genuine astronomers treated his so-called discoveries like a joke, and some publicly stated that with so many pieces of glass in the telescope, it would be so distorted that it would be impossible to see anything that had any resemblance to reality. Although we often say perhaps such claims as he may be right, in Bradbury's case, it is all so outlandish I think we can safely say the man was just fooling himself and anyone who took him seriously.

The Baboon That Ran A Railway

If you happened to be traveling by train in South Africa in the late 1800s and passed the signal box outside Cape Town, you might have seen something very strange – a baboon operating the signal switches. While it may have seemed like something in a circus or the planet of the Apes movie, it was actually a real situation.

A baboon named Jack was a highly intelligent animal who, for nine years, worked with the signalman as a trusted employee and as a friend.

The signalman was called James Wide and was nicknamed Jumper because in his younger days, working at the train depot, he used to jump between the railway carriages while they were slowly moving past until one day he slipped between two rail cars and was very badly injured. He eventually recovered but lost both his legs. He had a set of false legs, the classic peg legs like a pirate, and because he could not move around so quickly, he was given the job of controlling the signals for trains entering and leaving the station at Cape Town.

However, getting to work and back was still difficult for Jumper, and he made a small trolley cart to push himself around on. One day in the local market, he saw a man with a baboon, and the baboon was pulling a cart loaded with vegetables. Jumper had a great idea, and he bought the baboon from the man to help pull his cart so he could get to work and back home more easily.

Jumper named the baboon Jack, and Jack and Jumper became good friends.

Jack used to watch Jumper pulling the signal switches and one day tried to do it himself. Jumper had another bright idea, and he trained Jack to pull the appropriate switch levers depending on the incoming or outgoing trains.

Whenever a train entered or left the station or wanted to take a separate line to the fuel depot, the train driver would make the train give a series of whistles, and each whistle had a different meaning. Jumper trained Jack to recognize the whistles and pull the correct lever to switch the train onto the appropriate line.

Jack soon became adept at recognizing the train whistles and always pulled the correct lever so Jumper could just sit back and keep an eye on him. Jack had been working here for a couple of years when some passengers on a passing train saw a monkey operating the switches and were horrified - what if he pulled the wrong lever and caused a crash? The passenger complained to the railway authority, and Jumper and Jack were fired.

Jumper was heartbroken at losing his job, and he begged the railway authorities to reconsider. They eventually relented and said that Jack and Jumper would be reinstated, provided Jack could pass a test of his ability.

So, tests were arranged, and of course, Jack passed every test and proved his competence and safety. Jumper was given his job back, along with Jack, and they worked together for a total of nine years, with Jack never once making a mistake.

Sadly, Jack one day caught tuberculosis and died in 1890. The baboon, who had become well known and loved by all, was revered so much that his skull was kept and is still on display in a museum in Cape Town as a reminder of how intelligent some animals are.

Ants, Flies, And Pets, And Their Sense of Smell

We tend to think that dogs have the best sense of smell. It is true that dogs have a fantastic ability to smell from a long way away, but actually, the insect kingdom can give them a close run, size for size.

Ants actually have a very strong sense of smell and use it to find food. It is estimated that an ant can smell sugar from around 100 yards away. When you think how small an ant is compared to the average dog, it would be like a dog being able to smell food from 100 miles away – which, obviously, they can't.

Ants have their own body odor, called a pheromone, and all ant's pheromones are different. When two ants meet, they can sniff each other to find out if they come from the same colony or if they are strangers. Smell is also the ants' main method of communicating. For example, when they are looking for food, they leave a trail from their body odor for other ants to follow, which is why when you drop a piece of food on the ground, you will first get just one or two ants, then a whole line of them, following the trail left by the 'scouts.'

One unusual fact about ants is their love of roses. They love the smell and color of roses and just like to be near them, although they don't eat them – very rom*ant*ic!

The ordinary housefly is probably the star in the insect world when it comes to sniffing out food. Flies don't have actual noses, but they detect scents with their antennas and have been known to smell food from up to 7 kilometers away. This is a rare maximum, but normally, flies can smell something that attracts them from an average of 4 kilometers.

Of course, it helps that they are most attracted to really smelly stuff, like rotting garbage and other unpleasant things.

But the one that we are most familiar with is the dog. A pet dog has an incredible sense of smell compared to humans, and in their noses, they have about 300 million smell receptors, compared to humans, who have about 6 million. Nearly half a dog's brain is devoted to analyzing smells, and they are attracted to new and interesting odors.

In the perfect conditions, taking into account wind direction and the type of smell being produced, a dog can smell something up to 20 kilometers away, a distance that would take them 5 to 6 hours to walk, perhaps longer with rest stops. Of course, it would have to be a pretty strong smell to get a dog to travel 20 kilometers to find it!

But that is not the end of the story – cats can actually smell something up to 30 kilometers away. In general, cats have more smell receptors in their noses than dogs, with the exception of some types of dogs like Bloodhounds. Cats are all descended from fierce hunting creatures whose sense of smell was important in sniffing out danger and finding food in the wild. Cats are still natural hunters and will still go after mice and small birds, although now they don't really eat them.

Cats don't have much of a sense of taste and rely on scent to identify what food to eat. If you watch a cat closely, you will see that it will always sniff its food before tasting it. This is why, when a cat catches a cold, and its nose is a little blocked up, it can seem to lose its appetite and stop eating because it can't smell its food. They can get agitated by strong smells like aerosol sprays or people wearing a lot of perfume and will run off and not come back until the smell has gone.

All this information can be quite useful to know. We learn that it is important to always take care of garbage and not to leave food out without being covered. Ants and flies don't like the cold, so the fridge is the best place to keep the sort of food they are attracted to.

It's also worth knowing about dogs and cats to be able to care for them properly and understand what smells they like and don't like, and to make sure your cat is not in the room before you start spraying around air freshener.

Why Dogs Tilt Their Heads and Other Canine Facts

People love their dogs – that is a fact, and there are many reasons why. Dogs are loyal, protective, obedient (if trained well), and overall good companions. Dogs also do things that make them look cuter and more lovable, such as tilting their heads when they look at you as if they are listening to what you are saying. Experts think this is related to the dogs' hearing ability, which is helped by 'line of sight,' and tilting their head makes it easier to see past their muzzles, and they can hear better.

Did you know that dogs are partially color-blind? Researchers have found that all dogs only recognize the colors grey, brown, yellow, and blue. Doggy toys in bright reds, orange, or white may be attractive to humans, but to dogs, they are all the same dull colors. Although a dog's senses of smell and hearing are really excellent, their sight is not as good, and certainly not as good as cats, especially at night.

Why do dogs bury bones in the garden? This goes back to the days when they were wild animals and used to hunt for food, like wolves. Because they might go for a week or so without finding prey to eat, they would bury leftovers from their last meal to hide them from other animals, and the bones could be dug up again at a time when food was short. Strangely enough, this 'saving for later' instinct is still strong in the dog's subconscious, so they still do it today.

Is your dog left or right-handed?

You can usually tell, especially with a dog that has been trained to 'shake hands,' it will put its dominant paw out. Also, when a dog is playing with a toy or chewing on a large bone, it will use its dominant paw to hold the object steady. One interesting fact that researchers have found is that most dogs are right-handed, and they tend to dislike other dogs who are left-handed. You may sometimes see a dog growling at another one, and it could be because the other dog is left-handed, and the right-handed dogs can immediately sense that. Apparently, left-handed dogs also tend to be more aggressive. Those used as guide dogs, for example, are always right-handed because the trainers have found that left-handed dogs are not suitable and can be bad-tempered.

Dogs always seem to be hungry. Even after they have been fed, you can be sitting down to eat your own meal, and your dog will come alongside you like it is begging for food. Experts think that this comes from the time when humans sat around a campfire and used to throw scraps of food at their hunting dogs. The dogs never really got enough to make a decent meal, and hanging around humans when food is on the table is still a behavior that is hard-wired into the dogs, even if they are not hungry.

A dog is usually our closest animal companion, so it's a good idea to try to understand what they do and to realize that while humans have evolved a lot over the last few thousand years, much of a dog's behavior is still linked to their past.

The Mayan End of the World Prediction

The end of days, the great apocalypse, or the end of the world, have throughout history been regularly spoken about, and there have been many predictions about the end of the planet, none of which luckily have come true.

A very recent one was in the year 2012 when many people around the world believed that the ancient Mayan people had predicted the world would end on December 21, 2012. The Mayans were a very old civilization that existed in Central America long before Columbus landed, and they were quite advanced scientifically. They were so advanced that they had a calendar not only for days, weeks, and months but for years, in fact, covering centuries.

Their calendar, which was marked by symbols on stones and can be seen today, started in about 3,000 BC and went right up to 2012 when it ended, so it covered a period of 5,000 years. This was called by the Mayans a 'long count,' in their language a series of 400-year cycles called Baktun, and they did not count any further than 2012. Carved inscriptions that have been excavated at Mayan temple sites, although hard to understand, seemed to suggest that they predicted a God would descend and change the world. The prophecy did not say what would happen next.

Because the Mayans were known to be visionaries and were such advanced people, the belief spread around the world that the end date of the calendar - 12/21/12 - was when they thought the world would end. Groups of people prepared for the end by building retreats in unpopulated forest areas in the US, taking provisions and guns to survive whatever would happen. In Europe, people gathered on mountaintops in the hope that the God descending referred to an alien spacecraft that would come and rescue them. It all seems a bit crazy now, but at the time, it was taken very seriously by a lot of people.

Ideas were suggested that climate change would cause a worldwide disaster or perhaps an asteroid would collide with Earth. In the end, though, nothing really happened; the date came and went, and life went back to normal.

So, what was the fuss about the calendar all about? Experts now think that perhaps the Mayans ran out of numbers and the calendar was just intended to reset back to day zero again, just like in a car when the odometer that records the miles runs out of space and goes back to zero. Also, ending on December 21 might have been linked to the winter solstice, the day when night is longest, and after the 21st, the days get lighter in the evening.

Either way, just like all the other doomsday predictions, the world did not end (as you may have noticed). The only accurate prediction for the end of the planet is that in about 30 billion years, our sun will collapse and burn out, and the Earth will be destroyed in the process – but I don't think that is something we need to worry about, for a while at least.

The Real Secret of Area 51

There has always been a lot of mystery surrounding an American air force base known as Area 51. Many people believe that an alien spaceship crashed to Earth in the Nevada desert in the 1950s, and the remains were taken to Area 51 to be studied. Some people also think that an actual alien being was found in the spaceship, and its body has been preserved in a laboratory in Area 51. Over the years, there have been many such stories; people have claimed to see strange flying craft in the sky over the area, and all the conspiracy theories have been helped by the US government refusing to explain what goes on there, keeping Area 51 a big secret, and allowing no one to enter and have a look around.

However, recently, many secret documents have been declassified and made available to the public, and for the first time, we can all know exactly what the story is behind this hidden air base. It turns out that Area 51 was created so scientists could experiment with new aircraft technology in complete secrecy so that other countries, especially Russia and China, would not be able to spy on the latest developments. The fabled spacecraft crash was one of these experiments.

A new type of airplane was being developed using a metal called titanium, which made it almost undetectable to ordinary radar. This was the A12 plane, and it could fly at 2,200 miles an hour, able to cross the entire USA in 70 minutes. It flew at about three times the height of conventional aircraft at around 90,000 feet and also had very powerful cameras, which, even from that height, could give very detailed pictures of objects or even people on the ground. Unfortunately, the

A12 craft crashed during a test flight over the Nevada desert, and the government moved quickly to retrieve the wreckage and tried to pretend nothing happened. When some people said they had seen it, the government said it was just a weather balloon because they did not want other countries to find out what they were really doing. Of course, no one believed the weather balloon story, and the legend of a crashed spacecraft was born.

Test flights of similar new types of aircraft continued, which made people think they were seeing strange spaceships. The government was actually happy for people to believe these wild tales since it took attention away from their secret experiments.

Another plane developed in secret was the SR71, known as the Blackbird. This plane achieved a height of over 85,000 feet and flew from New York to London in about an hour and a half, flying at nearly 3 times the speed of sound. Other planes were designed as spy planes, hidden from radar, including the Suntan plane, which was fueled by liquid hydrogen.

Although the US government has now allowed documents about these experiments to be available to the public, it is thought that this is because all those craft are no longer in use and all work on them has finished. However, the air base at Area 51 is still in use, visitors are still not allowed, and whatever is happening there now is still top secret. It is likely that experts there are working on a completely new type of aircraft, but don't expect to hear anything about them, at least not for another 50 years. But one thing is certain: there never was any alien craft or spacemen at Area 51 – at least not according to the government, and of course, we believe them completely!

The New 7 Wonders of the World

When we hear about the 7 wonders of the world, we probably think about the ancient wonders that old Greeks and Romans built, among others. These old wonders were things like the Great Pyramid, the Colossus of Rhodes, the Hanging Gardens of Babylon, and the Great Temple of Artemis. Most of these, except for the pyramid, have gone now or have fallen into ruin, and in 1999, a Swiss organization called the New Wonders Foundation attempted to update the list and decided on what should now be the new 7 Wonders of the World. All great monuments and constructions were considered, and many were rejected, such as the Sydney Opera House and the Kremlin in Moscow. Other near contenders that ultimately did not make the final list were Stonehenge in England and the Eiffel Tower in Paris, France.

Out of 200 possible Wonders, it was finally narrowed down to 21, and then everyone in the world was invited to vote on what they thought should be the final 7. Nearly 100 million votes were counted, and the final 7 were chosen:

The 'Christ the Redeemer' Statue in Rio de Janeiro

This is a statue over 105 feet tall, built on top of Corcovado Mountain in Rio de Janeiro, Brazil. It took 9 years to construct, from 1922 to 1931, and it was completely renovated in 2010. There were around 630 tons of stone used to build the statue, and for a while, it was the biggest statue in the world, although now it is the third biggest.

The Great Wall of China

This wall was built over several centuries between the 5th and the 16th Century BC. It was built on the northern border of China to stop invasions by the Mongolian tribesmen, and it is the longest man-made structure in the world. It is said that it is the only structure on Earth that can be seen from outer space, and it stretches for around 4,000 miles.

The Colosseum in Rome

The Colosseum was built around 70 AD in Rome, Italy, and when finished, it could hold up to 50,000 people who came to watch a number of games and events. We all know about the gladiator fights and the mock battles, and there were also chariot races and displays of wild animals. Modern stadiums still use the same basic design as the Colosseum.

The City of Petra, Jordan

Famous from movies such as Indiana Jones, Petra was the ancient capital of a long-lost kingdom, Nabatea, in the Arabian Desert. It was carved into solid rose-colored rock and almost hidden in narrow canyons. It has many tall stone structures, such as a 140-foot-high temple, and in its day, it had water reservoirs, tunnels, and an arena that seated 4,000 people. It was abandoned for many centuries and was only discovered again by a Swiss explorer in 1812.

Machu Picchu, Peru

Machu Picchu dates back to the 15th century and was built on a nearly 8,000-foot-high mountain top in the Peruvian Amazon region, surrounded by jungle. It was part of the Inca civilization, and it is believed that when the Spanish invaded in the 1500s, many Inca people fled there to hide from the invaders. However, they brought with them new diseases they had caught from the Spanish conquistadores, like smallpox, which had previously been unknown in the country. As a result, the population was decimated, and the remaining survivors melted into the jungle and disappeared, leaving the city empty.

Chichen Itza, Mexico

Chichen Itza is a city that was built by the Mayan people and was the center of their civilization from 750 AD to 1200 AD. In the center of the city is the great Temple of Kukulkan, an 80-foot-high pyramid. The pyramid has four sides, and each side has 91 steps, totaling 364 representing each day of the year plus one more on top as a platform.

The Taj Mahal, Agra

Agra in India is home to this fantastic mausoleum, a huge burial monument built by the Indian emperor Shah Jehan for his wife, Mumtaz Mahal. The building was started in 1632 and was finished in 1646, taking 15 years to complete. It is recognized as one of the best examples of Indian architectural design from that era, and each year attracts millions of visitors.

Just thinking about all this, in hundreds of years' time, what do you think future generations will choose from our era as their new wonders? Or do we have anything that will last that long?

The Longest Living Creatures

What do you think are the oldest living creatures? Well, let's look at the list. Firstly, we think of elephants living a long time in the wild, and the oldest known elephant was 86 years old when it died. A macaw parrot was the oldest living bird at 106 years. In terms of people, the oldest known human was 122 years old. Some types of whales have been discovered to be able to survive for up to 230 years. One of the oldest animals was a tortoise, who lived to be 256.

But the oldest known living creature was found in 2007 in the Arctic Ocean and was a Quahog Clam. The clam's shell grows a new ring every year, and researchers have counted 405-year rings on this clam.

This means the clam was alive when William Shakespeare wrote his plays and was living when settlers first landed in America. Of course, the clam knew nothing about this or all the other world events over the more than 400 years it was alive since it lived in water 260 feet deep off the coast of Iceland.

Clams are known to live a long time. A previous record holder was a clam found in the sea around America in 1982, and it was 220 years old. Another clam from Iceland was later found to be 374 years old.

Technically speaking, the oldest creature on the planet is coral. While we may think of a piece of coral as just a sort of rock, it is actually a living creature, although personally, I would classify it alongside mushrooms or fungus or maybe a sort of plant. But scientists definitely say it is a living creature, even though it just looks like an underwater stone.

Having said that, some corals are known to have existed for over 5,000 years, and if scientists are right, then they are certainly the oldest living creatures on the planet. Coral fossils, the ancestors of today's corals, have been found that are 240 million years old, which means that coral existed on the planet millions of years before people.

Corals are made up of hundreds of thousands of small creatures called polyps, which eat plankton, the microscopic things in the water that whales also eat. Corals can also move around, although it takes them years to move a few feet.

The longest-living mammal is a type of whale – the Bowhead whale – which can live for several hundred years. The reason it lives a long time is that it has a type of gene that protects it from disease and also another gene that is responsible for cell growth and repair to damaged cells. Scientists have been studying the Bowhead whale for a while in the hope that they can isolate these genes and perhaps apply them to humans, although I am really not sure if I would want to live more than 200 years – would you? Plus, the planet would get so overcrowded with old people we would all go crazy.

Anyway, going back to the clam, if you are wondering what happened to it, well, it was still alive when it was taken out of the water, but unfortunately, it did not survive during the time its rings were being counted. That seems a bit unfair, considering that if it had been left alone, it might have lived for another couple of hundred years, but we will never know.

Animals That Use Tools

For a long time, everyone believed that only humans used tools in daily life, especially to find or make food. It was thought that this was one of the ways that separated people from animals. However, in recent years, it has been discovered that many animals use tools for food and even for survival.

In the bird kingdom, we all know that birds build their nests with twigs and leaves, but it is not widely known that some birds use objects for other reasons. For example, crows use small twigs to get their food. They have been seen to pick up twigs and use them to get at grubs and insects in the bark of trees and have even been seen to break longer twigs into shorter pieces to make them easier to handle with their beaks.

Orangutans will often make a whistling noise to warn others in their tribe when predators like snakes are near. Sometimes, they will take leaves from tree branches and whistle by blowing through the leaves. Animal researchers have found that they do this to make the whistling sound deeper, as if from a bigger animal, to try to frighten the predators away. Experts say this is the only case they know of where an animal uses a tool to make a sound.

Another species of monkey, the macaque, lives in Thailand. They are a popular tourist attraction, especially around Buddhist temples, and will often pull hairs from tourists' heads, especially long hairs. What the tourists don't realize is that the macaques use the long hairs as dental floss to keep their teeth clean!

Sea otters are known to use stones to knock shellfish off rocks and then use the stones to break open the shells so they can eat what is inside. A type of fish in Australia does something similar. The fish picks up some shellfish in its mouth and hits it against a rock until the shell breaks open. Dolphins also use tools to find food.

They can pick up sponges off the seabed and use them to stir up the sand at the bottom of the ocean to try to uncover their prey.

What is really interesting about these creatures is that they don't just decide to use a tool themselves; they are taught how to do it. Older animals, on land and on sea, have been discovered teaching younger animals how to use tools. Perhaps one day, scientists will discover animal schools where using tools is the main lesson!

Gold Comes From Outer Space

We tend to think that all the metals we have today, like iron, silver, and tin, have always been part of the planet. But there is one metal that does not belong on Earth. In fact, it first came from outer space, which is gold. Gold has always been seen as a precious and valuable commodity, and the fact that we have been able to dig it out of the ground makes us think that it has been there since the planet was first formed. If you ask most people where gold comes from, they will say out of a goldmine or in a river bed. However, gold itself is actually older than our solar system and was around long before our planet.

To understand this, we need to look back to when the universe was first formed. Stars were exploding and colliding with each other, producing clouds of gas and dust, which were caught in the orbits of other stars and gradually became solid planets. Other stars grew to enormous size and exploded in nuclear explosions, throwing millions of tons of different materials into space. The metal gold was formed in these explosions and was sent through the universe, and some landed on Earth, so in fact, gold was formed from dead stars. At that time, billions of years ago, the Earth was not as solid as it is now, and the heavy gold metal sank deep into the Earth's crust. Various earthquakes and other disturbances on the planet pushed some gold closer to the top of the crust, where today it can be found.

To prove how this happened, scientists can actually make gold using nuclear energy reactors, but the cost of making a small amount of gold this way is hundreds of times more expensive than the value of the gold itself, so it is not something they do very often, and anyway, there is enough gold already undiscovered on the planet. It is estimated that so far, throughout history, around 196,000 tons of gold have been found, but in fact, it is believed that there are still about 1 million tons of gold in the Earth's crust.

Gold is not just made into jewelry or kept in banks in gold bars; it is in nearly everything we use today. All computers and cell phones contain gold, and it is also used in coatings for sunglasses because, unlike other metals, gold does not react with oxygen, so it never rusts or tarnishes, and it is also the best conductor of electricity. You can even eat gold-covered chocolate! Doctors still inject patients with gold to treat arthritis, and dentists use it as tooth fillings.

So, if you ever have a gold ring or maybe a necklace, or even if you are using a cell phone, you should remember that not only is it a valuable and beautiful metal, but it is also a gift from the stars.

The Oldest Living Tree

Trees are useful objects and, throughout history, have been used for everything from building houses and furniture to sailing ships and even weapons of war, like the giant catapults used by the Romans. Where would we be without trees? Not only are they our most useful natural resource, but they also provide most of the oxygen on the planet. The vast rainforests of Asia and South America give us the air that we breathe.

Normally, we think of an old tree as being a few hundred years old, but in fact, there are many trees that are much older. A tree in the Waipoua forest in New Zealand is 2,000 years old, and a tree called The Senator in Florida is 3,500 years old.

Even older is a tree in the Inyo forest in California called Methuselah, which is 4,765 years old. But the oldest living tree, discovered in Sweden in 2004, is actually 9,550 years old.

The tree itself is not that old, however. It is a Norway Spruce tree, the type we use as a Christmas Tree, and it could be used for that if your house is big enough because it is only 13 feet high, but the roots of the tree are over 9,500 years old.

The trunk of the tree has a life of around 600 years, after which it starts to die off, and a new trunk sprouts from the root system like a clone, keeping the tree alive. Other 'Christmas trees' have also been found in Sweden that are between 5,000 and 6,000 years old, but the oldest is the original Norway Spruce, and there cannot be a tree older than that in the Northern hemisphere because most of the land was covered in a sheet of ice until the Ice Age ended about 11,000 years ago.

All the trees in Europe were originally just low-growing shrubs in the mountain tundra areas during the ice age, and as the ice melted, it transplanted seeds from the shrubs over the whole area, which over thousands of years developed into huge forests in the lower levels of the mountain areas.

In the Southern Hemisphere, the climate was always a little warmer, and researchers think that trees were growing in forests on the Australian island of Tasmania more than 10,000 years ago. However, it is unlikely that you will find a tree much older than 10 years in your town. Trees in towns and cities have a short life expectancy due to pollution, but overall, trees are still the longest-living things on the planet, and we would not survive without them. They provide shelter and food for a variety of animals, and they help to keep our air clean. One acre of trees can remove as much carbon pollution from the air as could be caused by a car being driven nearly 9,000 miles.

As well as being some of the oldest, the trees in California are also some of the tallest. The biggest known tree is a Redwood tree measuring 360 feet high, which is about 200 school desks stacked on top of each other!

Entrance to the Underworld

Most civilizations that have ever existed on Earth have had their own ideas of Gods and spirits, and generally, they still do. Many of them also believed in their own versions of heaven and hell, and many superstitions were built around these ideas. While they all generally agreed that you would go to heaven after dying, provided you lived a good life, many civilizations also believed that you could go to hell while still on Earth; in fact, there were many places that were regarded as the entrances to hell or the underworld as it was called.

These were real places on the planet, and they still exist, so anyone can visit them today to see what the ancient people thought was the entrance to hell. Here are the top ten best-known entrances to the underworld from all over the world.

Sybil's Cave

Sybil was a famous priestess from Greek and Roman times, known for being able to foresee the future and tell people their fortune. She also acted as a guide to the underworld and could take people into her cave to seek out their departed loved ones like a modern psychic medium. The cave is located at a place called Cumae, near modern Naples, and is a labyrinth of twisting underground tunnels.

The Ghost City of Fengdu

This is a city in ancient China that was supposedly ruled by the king of hell, where demons guarded a bridge that led to the underworld. Fengdu is featured in many Chinese stories and legends, and the tales tell that a spirit had to pass three tests before being allowed to cross the bridge. The city is now a major tourist attraction, and actors re-enact the bridge crossing to the afterlife.

Pluto's Gate

In olden times, Pluto was not a Disney cartoon character but the Roman god of the underworld. His gate was in a place called Hierapolis, which was located in what is now Turkey. It is actually still a dangerous place because it is a small stone room built over a cave that constantly emits carbon dioxide from deep underground, and anyone staying too long in the stone chamber would be suffocated.

Castle Houska

This old castle was built in the mid-1200s, and the story is that it was built over the entrance to hell. The Christian chapel of the castle is supposedly directly over the gate to hell and was built to stop demons from escaping from a pit below the castle. It is often visited by people interested in the supernatural, although the actual pit has never been found.

St. Patrick's Cellar

St. Patrick was the patron saint of Ireland, and his cellar or cave is located on an island just off the coast. It was a place of pilgrimage, with many people journeying there to see what was described as St. Patrick's Purgatory, a place in between heaven and hell. Apparently, people could go there and see both places they may go to after they die and possibly decide which they would prefer. The cave is now closed off to the public, but religious people still believe the story and visit the site every year.

Guinee Gates

Based on Voodoo religious beliefs, Guinee is the place where the dead go while they wait to be with their ancestors, and it is ruled by the lord of the dead, Baron Samedi. There are seven gates to Guinee, all located around the city of New Orleans, and to get into the gates, the spirits have to visit each one in the correct order. Each gate has a guardian who must be given a specific gift, and if the rituals are not done correctly, the demons will carry the spirits off to hell.

Lake of Avernus

The Avernus Lake is a large body of water in an old volcanic crater in Southern Italy, which the Romans believed could be used as an entrance to the underworld. They built temples and bathhouses around the lake, and it was especially popular with very old people or sick people who believed their time of death was near so they could be close to their eventual destination.

Hekla Mountain

This is an active volcano in Iceland, which has regularly erupted since the year 1104 when ash and rock thrown up by the volcano covered half the country. People at the time thought this was the entrance to hell, and flocks of birds disturbed by the eruption were thought to be the souls of the dead. Hekla is still occasionally erupting and is a popular spot for hikers to visit.

Mount Osore

This is another volcano, this time in Japan, and although it has not erupted in the last 10,000 years, it still emits clouds of smoke and steam. There is a temple on the mountain where pilgrims believe they can contact the spirits of the dead, and near the temple is the Sanzu River, which legend says can carry souls to the underworld.

The River Acheron

The Acheron River in Greece is only 32 miles long, which is quite short for a river, and according to the ancient Greeks, it is one of the five rivers of the underworld that the souls of the dead have to cross.

It was also claimed to have healing powers for the living and is still visited today by sick people hoping for a miracle cure.

Of course, you should not be afraid to visit any of these places today because they are not really entrances to the underworld… or are they?

Your Brains Can Sleep While you are Awake

When we sleep, our brains switch off, and they are always active while we are awake – or at least that is what we always think. Actually, the complete opposite can often be the truth. At night, during sleep, our brains produce vivid dreams and sorts out our memory and experiences from the previous day, which we probably already knew anyway. What we might not have already known is that sometimes the brain goes to sleep when we are awake, which sounds like it should be impossible, but it really happens.

Scientists have been observing electrical activity in the brains of people who have been forced to go without sleep for long periods, and they have found that parts of the brain fall into something called 'local sleep.' Despite this, there was no way to tell from outside that the brain was asleep – the subjects of the experiments behaved completely normally except when it came to solving simple problems or making decisions because that was the part of the brain that had gone to sleep.

In normal sleep, the nerve cells, called neurons, in the brain that collect and transmit signals around the brain and the body slow right down, and on a brain monitor, are shown as slow wave patterns. This stage of sleep accounts for 80% of all sleep in people and animals. After keeping the subjects awake for extended periods when they would normally be sleeping, it was found that neurons in two important sections of the brain entered into a slow-wave pattern, which was basically sleep, although the subjects were fully awake.

Researchers believe that our brains are always in control, and even though we may want to stay awake, for example, on a long journey or during an exciting event, the brain still needs to turn itself off to stop recording new information, to process existing information, and to reset itself for a new day. What this means is that even though we feel awake and alert, we can make stupid mistakes and bad decisions that we would not normally make. This can be the cause of traffic accidents, and it has been found that this state of 'brain sleep' is the same as when a person has drunk alcohol – everything seems fine, but there is a loss of judgment.

Adults generally need 7 to 9 hours of sleep every 24 hours, and although some people say they only need a few hours' sleep, it is probable that during the day, parts of their brains are sleeping anyway.

This is especially true of school kids who spend all night playing video games. When they are at school the next day, they may have difficulty learning and remembering their lessons, not because they are stupid, but because their brains are basically asleep, which is a great excuse to give your teacher!

Crows Are As Smart As People

Traditionally, we have thought that the animals with the closest intelligence to humans are the monkeys, mainly because they are almost human-like creatures, and there is a generally accepted theory that we evolved from a species of ape. There is another animal, though, that displays an intelligence level similar to humans, and that is a bird, the crow.

Crows are some of nature's smartest birds. They can make tools, play tricks on each other, and even have conversations amongst themselves. These are just some of the behaviors that show a similarity between crows and people, such as being able to identify danger from other birds or from humans and being able to communicate that to other birds nearby to warn them. This is especially the case when crows see a human; they watch carefully to see if the person will be a threat, and they will let other crows know about it.

When it comes to using tools, crows are very advanced in the animal kingdom. A study at Oxford University in England found that crows can solve problems faster than other animals, including chimps. When trying to get a container of food out of a tube, they were able to bend a piece of wire into a hook to pull the food out, which means they were able to work out in their minds the best way to solve the problem and then do it. Crows, like humans, also live in families with an average of four – mum, dad, and two kids.

It has been estimated that crows have the intelligence level of a 7-year-old human child, which might not be astounding, but it puts them above most other animals, including cats and dogs, especially when it comes to problem-solving. In one study at the University of

Auckland in New Zealand, crows were given a jug of water and a pile of stones. The water level was too low for the crows to reach and drink, so the crows picked up the stones in their beaks and dropped them into the jug to raise the water level until they could reach it.

Crows also have long memories and can teach other crows what they know. For example, there is a town in Ontario, Canada, where up to half a million crows would stop over on their annual migration route until the townspeople got tired of damage to their crops and started shooting at the crows to scare them off. It worked, and for generations, crows have not stopped off at the town, just flying straight past, although they always deposit their droppings on the town as they pass overhead – which may or may not be their version of revenge. But it shows that they let all the other crows know that it was a dangerous place to stop.

Crows hide food to eat later, but if they see another bird watching them, they will fly off to another spot where they will not be observed. They have also adapted to modern traffic; they have been seen to drop nuts on a roadway to be cracked open bypassing cars, and they do this at crossings controlled by traffic lights because they know that when the lights are red, the traffic will stop and it is safe to fly down and collect the nuts. Crows have even been known to memorize garbage days, so they know when people put out their garbage on the street, and they can swoop down to see if there is anything worth eating.

This is remarkable because even some humans cannot remember when garbage day is!

The World's Oldest Mattress

A story about an old bed may not sound very interesting, but this one gives an insight into how people lived tens of thousands of years ago. It is a mattress that was found in a cave in South Africa and is estimated to be around 77,000 years old. It is about 22 feet square, and it seems the cave dwellers all slept together on one bed as a family rather than have separate beds. This could have been for warmth or safety or just because it was comfortable. Or perhaps it was too much trouble to make more than one bed.

The bed is actually in layers. Apparently, they never threw out an old bed and made a new one; they just regularly laid more material over the top of the old stuff as it got a bit worn out, resulting in the bed being around 12 inches high, higher than most modern mattresses.

The mattress was made of layers of reeds and rushes, and since there was no other furniture, the assumption is that the bed was also where the cave people ate their meals, so they had breakfast in bed every morning.

On top of the reeds and rushes, there were layers of leaves and grasses for comfort, and on the top was a layer of leaves from a type of laurel tree known to have insect-killing properties, so the cave dwellers had discovered a way to keep the bed bugs away. Native groups in Africa still use the leaves of the laurel tree to keep insects away, a practice passed down over tens of thousands of years.

This high, well-made mattress would have been very comfortable and would have lasted a long time, showing that the early humans valued their sleep after a long day hunting saber-tooth tigers or whatever. Actually, the earliest humans who first evolved around 2 million years ago slept in trees like monkeys for safety and did not move into caves until the discovery of fire. When they did, the first thing they did was to look for ways to get a decent night's sleep, and so they developed the mattresses.

These early cave-dwelling humans were small people, much smaller than we are today on average, and certainly not as well-fed, so a large bed like this one would have been able to accommodate several generations together – children, parents, grandparents, even uncles, and aunties would have all been able to fit on a bed this size.

The concept of a comfortable bed has not changed much over time, although, of course, they are made from different materials now. It is said that choosing a mattress is one of the most important decisions you will make because sleep is so important to our bodies, and it seems the early cave people in Africa certainly knew that.

Music Makes The Brain Work Better

It has always been known that music can affect our brains. From the loud and violent pounding of a rock concert for a massive audience to the more respectable and peaceful symphony for a hall of classical music lovers, music can both stimulate and relax the brain. In the past, there has been a lot of research into how this works, and recent studies have looked at how music can have a direct effect on certain parts of the brain, including the part that deals with language. All humans in the world have those two things in common: music and language, so it is no surprise that they are connected in the brain.

Playing music has been found to help people hear better, in general. The brains of people who learn or are learning to play a musical instrument such as a piano have been found to be better able to hear other sounds, like people talking in a noisy environment like a party or a disco. This is part of the link between music and language.

Music can also be used as a medicine, and musical therapy has been practiced for nearly 100 years. It is claimed to help people with brain disorders such as anxiety or depression and even major illnesses like Parkinson's or Alzheimer's Disease. Music produces chemicals in the brain that change moods and assist memory, as well as relaxes emotions. When music is played, it produces a sound wave, and when brain waves are measured during the playing of music, the brain waves are found to be exactly the same as the sound waves, almost as if the music is playing the brain.

This is especially important for people who have problems like dyslexia or ADHD and who have problems concentrating in noisy environments like school classrooms, etc. Music therapy and learning to play an instrument help them to overcome the problems because they are linked to language ability.

It even works with people who have no musical ability and start to learn to play the drums. Older people and those in particular who have had a stroke or have difficulty moving around find that their body movements become better after trying to play drums, and it helps people to stop shaking.

The research shows that listening to music can improve the quality of your sleep and reduce blood pressure and anxiety, as well as help to improve mental alertness, which is why a lot of people listen to music while driving, especially long distances, to keep their minds active.

The type of music is also important, especially for older people. Medical experts say that older folk should listen to the same music that the kids enjoy. Although it can be comforting for people to listen to the sort of music they are familiar with from their youth years ago, the brain works better when it is challenged, and it improves the brain processes when it struggles to come to terms with the sounds of new and unfamiliar music.

So, when you hear older people say they can't understand today's music, tell them it's probably because they haven't been listening enough, and they should try harder because it's good for their brains!

When Lambs Grew on Trees

Anyone who has ever gone past a sheep farm will have seen little lambs skipping through the fields, watched closely by their mothers, and obviously, you can tell that they were born as baby lambs, like all mammals. But there was a time in history when everyone thought that lambs actually grew on trees like some sort of meaty fruit.

The period we know as the Middle Ages was from 500 AD to 1400 AD, and it was a time when people really did not know much about why things happened in nature, so they made up stories to fit the situation, and their world was full of mistakes and superstitions. Nowadays, our understanding of science and nature is much more knowledgeable, but in those olden days, it seemed quite reasonable to believe that a certain type of lamb grew on trees.

Of course, they knew that not all lambs grew on trees – that would be crazy, right? But as people traveled from West to East, exploring the trade routes from Europe all the way through the Arab countries to India and China, they saw some strange sights and came back home after their travels with some wild tales. One of these stories concerned amazing trees growing in Tartary – which was the name in those days for an area of Central Asia, North West of China, now mostly Mongolia – on which grew a type of lamb.

This was not just one odd traveler's tale; the lamb tree was well-known and was written about in many books dating from that time. There were descriptions of the tree and the lambs, even descriptions of how it tasted. The lambs were said to be hanging from the trees like large fruit and were definitely growing on vines.

Because most of these books recorded a consistent story, the travelers must have seen something that looked like a lamb growing on a tree. Some writers who said that they had eaten this lamb said it tasted a bit like chicken, and others said it was like a fish.

In fact, it might have been discovered much earlier, in the time of the ancient Greeks, when the legend of Jason and the Argonauts was a popular story. Jason supposedly traveled to a distant land where he found a lamb's fleece – the Golden Fleece – growing on a tree. Or it could have just been a misunderstanding since the ancient Greek word was lamb, which was the same as the word for melon.

As the centuries progressed and people became more aware of their natural world, most people started to be skeptical that an actual animal could grow on a tree like an apple, and eventually, in 1600, a specimen of a strange plant was brought to London by a member of the Royal Society. It was a large gourd-like plant about 12 inches long, covered in a downy growth-like hair, with several bits sticking out like legs, and it could be eaten like a potato. This was a Fern Rhizome, a plant native to parts of China, and was probably the lamb that people saw growing on trees.

Nowadays, people are much more skeptical and are not likely to believe every crazy story they hear – unless it is on the internet!

The Invention of Fireworks

Fireworks are always very popular at celebrations and events, usually rounding off an evening of entertainment with a great fireworks display of bright colors, explosions, and wonderful shapes. Not long ago, anyone could buy fireworks to set off at home for their own fireworks parties, and in some places, they were sold all year round and not just on special occasions. These days, because of the dangers, the sale of fireworks is restricted, and to see a fireworks show, you have to go to a special event. But where did fireworks come from?

It all started in ancient China, where not only fireworks but also gunpowder was invented around the same time. People in those days were very superstitious and thought that evil spirits came to frighten them at night, so they dug pits around their houses and lit fires in the pits. To make the flames bigger and noisier, they tried throwing different things into the fire pits, and they found that things like charcoal, Sulphur, and potassium together made loud bangs and created showers of sparks when burnt.

They refined the mixture and found that if they packed it tightly in bamboo poles, it was even more explosive when alight. This was the start of the invention of gunpowder and of course, the gun as a weapon. Because the bamboo firework poles made such loud noises and made colorful explosions, people gradually stopped using them just to frighten away spirits and started to use them as entertainment. Well – who doesn't like loud bangs and colored sparks?

After a while, they began to experiment by adding metal shaving and iron filings, which made fantastic patterns and showers of bright sparks in the sky, and fireworks were used at every celebration, including weddings.

Travelers from Europe who came to trade with the Chinese brought the mysterious exploding substance back with them, and it was not long before they developed rockets and missiles they could fire at their enemies. Out of this was invented the musket and eventually cannons and smaller guns. At the same time, they used gunpowder to create more interesting and amazing fireworks, which were displayed at royal occasions, big parties, and major religious events.

In the late 1700s, settlers in America declared their independence from England, and the date of the Declaration of Independence was celebrated with wonderful fireworks shows. John Adams, one of the founding fathers and the 2nd US president, liked the fireworks displays so much that he decreed that the 4th of July should always be celebrated with fireworks, and it always has.

However, the fireworks they had in those days were still just loud bangs and showers of sparks, and the type of fireworks we know today were developed in Italy in the mid-1800s when two families who manufactured fireworks experimented with making different shapes and colors to light up the sky. Later in the 1880s, both families emigrated to America, taking the secrets of their fantastic fireworks with them, and over time, these have become the fireworks we know today.

In those days, there was always a bit of a risk with fireworks, and many people were injured trying to use them. These days, they are much safer and more sophisticated, and most firework displays are controlled by computers – there is probably even a firework app.

The Lost World of Atlantis

Of all the mysteries in the world, one of the best known is the story of Atlantis – a marvelous city in an advanced civilization that existed for thousands of years and then suddenly disappeared.

The lost city of Atlantis is featured in movies and books and has been the subject of expeditions searching for the wonderful place, with explorers convinced it really existed and is now somewhere under the ocean. The name of the Atlantic Ocean, by the way, is not connected to Atlantis. The word Atlantic comes from the Greek Word' Atlas', who was a figure in Greek Mythology who supported the world on his shoulders.

Atlantis was first mentioned by the Greek writer Plato in 360 BC, and he described it as a great military power and a highly advanced civilization that had disappeared in a terrible event, possibly a great flood or Earthquake. Other ancient historians also claimed to have heard about the place. The Roman writer, Marcellinus accompanied Julius Caesar on his campaigns in Gaul. Marcellinus wrote that the Gaul Druids had told him that they were descended from a race of people that came out of the sea and that their homeland had been destroyed in a great flood and was now underwater. Marcellinus took this to mean that the inhabitants of the area originally came from the lost Atlantis, which was now submerged under the sea.

In the 1500s, at least two writers came up with theories that Atlantis was originally located in the Americas and that the Mayan and Aztec peoples were descended from the Atlanteans. Thomas More and Francis Bacon both argued that this was how the early American people, like the Mayans, were able to build pyramids and had knowledge of mathematics and astronomy that was unknown in the Western world because they had the knowledge passed down from a more sophisticated civilization.

The theories got a boost in the 1800s. Writers and historians began looking at the achievements of some countries in metalworking and architecture and thought that the people involved were just not able to come up with this knowledge on their own because their civilizations were not very advanced, so the ability to create and understand how to do these things must have been passed down from somewhere, and the idea of Atlantis fitted the theory. They supposed that the world of Atlantis must have been destroyed in the flood mentioned in the bible, which covered the whole world, and only Noah and his family survived.

One of the modern-day theories is that Atlantis was located in the Caribbean Sea, in the part known as the Bermuda Triangle. This is one explanation for the strange occurrences around the Triangle, and some people believe they are due to the power of Atlantis deep underwater. Another theory is that Atlantis was in the Antarctic area millions of years ago before it became frozen over.

However, my favorite theory is that Plato just made it all up – he was a writer, and he wrote an interesting story that many other people throughout history have actually believed. I think this is probably the most likely explanation for the lost city of Atlantis, and so far, no one has found any evidence to contradict this theory.

Inventions from the Middle Ages

We think of the Middle Ages as being a primitive time, hundreds of years ago, when people did not know much about the world and were subject to a lot of wars and plagues when they weren't starving or dying in childbirth. It was a difficult time for the average person, and life was tough.

However, it will surprise you to learn that even in those early times, there were smart people who invented things we still use today. One example of this is the clock. Not the digital clock you have beside your bed or the battery-driven clock on the wall of your lounge, but the mechanical clock, the wind-up type.

For a long time, they used water clocks, sundials, and marked candles to tell the time, but these were not very reliable and could only tell the approximate hour of the day. Then, in 1510, a German, Peter Heinlen, came up with a spring-driven mechanical clock that could tell time in minutes and seconds. At first, not many people saw the need to know the time accurately, but soon, it was adopted by monks in monasteries as a way of knowing their prayer times and checking exactly how long they would pray for.

After a while, the idea spread around the world, and soon, everyone wanted a mechanical clock ticking away in their house. The basic design is still used today, especially in expensive watches that are spring-driven rather than rely on batteries.

Another invention from the Middle Ages is eyeglasses. It was known for at least 1,000 years that looking through curved glass would make objects look bigger, or if you looked the other way, they were smaller. But it was not until about the mid-1300s that an Italian designer came up with a way of making small round pieces of glass in a framed holder that helped people to see better.

Again, it was the monks who were the first major users of these new glasses since they spent many long hours writing and illustrating religious texts and books. The basic design of eyeglasses has not changed much since then, although the development of the lenses has become more accurate for different people's needs.

Another development from the Middle Ages is paper money. Early civilizations used shells or beads or just a barter system, where, for example, a man would go to market with a cow and exchange it in barter for two pigs. However, there were times when a person had something of value but did not want to exchange it for anything at that moment but would do so later, in which case he could sell the cow for silver coins, which he could use to buy something at another time.

When it got to the stage that people had to carry around a lot of coins, someone had the idea that they could keep the coins safe in a bank, which would give them a piece of paper saying it was worth so many silver coins and that could be used to buy things. Paper money was first used in China around 1100 AD and spread to Europe in about 1500.

One of the greatest inventions that changed the world was actually the idea of public libraries. Before those times, not many people knew how to read, mainly because books were very scarce and valuable. They were always hand-written and used mainly by religious orders and the nobility.

In 1473, however, William Caxton invented the printing press, and printed books became available, although the general public still did not have access to them. About 100 years later, after I suppose enough books had been printed, public libraries were developed where anybody could come and read a book.

At first, no one was allowed to take a book out of the library until 1608, when the first lending library opened in Norwich, England. With the availability of books, there was more interest in learning to read, and this started to change all of society and led to the popularity of newspapers, songsheets, books, and authors.

So don't let anyone tell you that medieval times were full of primitive people living in mud houses – they invented many of the things that changed the world.

Creatures That Never Grow Old

You probably know the story of Peter Pan, the boy who never grew up. But that is just fiction, and in real life, we all grow older. Our cells are constantly dividing and renewing, and over time, this process slows down, so we have fewer new cells every day, and the old ones, well, they just get older. This aging process is common to just about all life on the planet – insects, animals, and plants – but there are some species where this does not happen.

For some creatures, they produce enzymes – chemicals in their bodies – that keep the cells renewing themselves so that they never grow older.

One example of this is a sea creature called a Hydra. It is a very simple life form. Basically, a long tube with a mouth at one end and a foot on the other, which they use to attach themselves to a rock on the seabed and grab passing microscopic prey. The Hydra's cells appear to have an infinite capacity to renew themselves, so as soon as the Hydra reaches a level of maturity, it stops growing and stays there, possibly forever. It's all down to a gene in their bodies called the FoxO genes, and scientists have experimented by removing this gene from the Hydra in an aquarium and found that they then start to age and wither away.

Another more well-known creature that never grows older is the lobster. You might be aware that what we see as lobsters is actually just a shell. The real lobster is inside, and every year, it gets a bit bigger, so it has to leave that shell and grow a new one, which is quite an amazing process by itself. Anyway, the actual lobster produces an enzyme called telomerase. We all have this, and humans and most animals have less and less every year as we get older.

However, the lobster has the same amount of telomerase all the time, so it never ages and keeps outgrowing its shell. Unfortunately, though, the lobster doesn't live forever. It takes a huge amount of energy to build a new shell, and sooner or later, the lobster just gets tired and can't be bothered and basically just collapses, and that is the end of the lobster.

It's not just creatures that don't get older.

Various tree species have been found to not age, like the aspens in Utah, USA. Although the actual trees are only about 150 years old, it is believed that their huge underground root system, which continually grows more trees, is up to 80,000 years old, dating back to the last Ice Age.

So, why is the whole world not full of creatures and plants that never age? Well, the answer is that although they don't get older, they can still get attacked by other creatures. The long-lived Hydra gets nibbled at bypassing fish, and of course, the lobsters' biggest predator is man, who sees the crustacean as a tasty treat. As for plants and trees, they are preyed on by insects and forest dwellers, and again, man is the biggest predator. When ships were made out of wood, millions of trees were cut down to build them, and even now, people cut down and burn huge areas of forest to plant crops.

There may come a time when people will stop getting older; scientists are constantly experimenting with the genes and enzymes from some of these creatures to see what effect they would have on us. One day, people might be able to live forever, but would you want to? Maybe, just like the lobster, we would run out of energy and just give up!

Cats Don't Eat Sweets

If you own a cat as a pet, there is one thing you might know about them, or if you don't know, you should find out – cats don't eat anything sweet. It is not because they are sensible and do not want to put on weight or have tooth decay. It is just that they don't have the taste receptor in their mouths that lets them taste anything sweet. This makes them unique among all the mammals on the planet. The only other creature that cannot taste anything sweet is the chicken, but they are birds, not mammals.

Humans obviously can taste sweets. Although many people try to avoid eating sugar, they still get natural sweetness in fruit and many other foods because it is a prime source of energy. What happens is that when we taste something sweet, the taste receptors on our tongues send a signal to the brain that tells our brain that it is an indication of carbohydrates, which we need to get through the day and build strength in our bodies, so the brain sends back a signal to say, "great - let's have some more!" That is because, like many animals, we are omnivorous, which means we eat everything and anything.

Cats, however, are strictly carnivorous – they eat only meat. This applies to all cats, not just your little kitty, but also to the big cats, lions, tigers, etc. Since they first evolved, cats have been hunters, and even inside your household, this pet is a killer waiting to get out and hunt for a mouse or bird.

Of course, many cats are fed dried cat food, but it is always meat-based or meat-flavored. It is not that cats don't like anything sweet; they just can't taste it. If you give your cat a piece of chocolate candy, it might eat it out of curiosity, but it won't taste anything and will be a bit like if you chew on a piece of plain cardboard.

Cats actually don't have much interest in many types of food. They only want meat. Dogs, of course, will eat anything, and this is because they have about 1,700 taste receptors in their mouths, whereas cats only have 470. Humans, by comparison, have over 9,000, which is one reason why many people always want to try new and interesting flavors from around the world, and why there are so many different types of restaurants, all designed to tempt our 9,000 taste buds.

In many cases, cats have been known to eat ice cream or even doughnuts, but that is because they can detect fat in them, which is a major component in meat. So, if you are eating a peanut butter and jelly sandwich, your pet dog will be hanging around hoping to get a tasty morsel, whereas your cat just won't be interested at all and will probably carry on either hunting or sleeping, the two main activities of all cats, large and small, everywhere in the world.

More Lego Figures Than People and Other Lego Facts

If you love Lego, you might be interested to know that the first Lego figure was made in 1978 and was a Lego policeman. Since then, there have been billions of Lego figures made, and it is estimated that there are more Lego people than real people in the world today. Lego figures are all made to an exact size, all the same at 4 Lego bricks tall.

Lego brick measurements are so precise because they all have to fit together, and only 18 out of every million are rejected as not good enough. There is even Lego in space; in 2011, NASA launched the Juno spaceship, a probe rocket destined for the planet Jupiter. On board, there were no people, but there was a set of Lego figures that set the record for the furthest distance traveled by a piece of Lego.

Now, that would be very interesting if aliens happened to come across the spaceship –would they think the Lego figures looked like people on Earth?

The most expensive Lego figure ever made was a solid gold figure modeled on Boba Fett from the Star Wars movies and TV series. Only two were ever made from 14-carat gold, and they are each valued at around $12,000. They were made as special prizes at a world comic book convention – the San Diego Comic-Con.

Lego is one of the most popular toys in the world, and there are 36,000 Lego bricks being made every minute. It is estimated that there are currently around 400 million Lego bricks, which, if all stacked on top of each other, would be about 2.5 million miles high, which is ten times higher than the moon. However, the tallest Lego tower on

Earth is just 114 feet tall, which is still an amazing feat, and was built in Milan in, Italy in 2015 using about 500,000 Lego bricks. The number of Lego pieces made in one year, if laid end to end, would circle the Earth 5 times.

If you have any Lego, you will know they fit together in many different ways.

Although there are many small bits of Lego in a set, the standard piece has 8 little plastic studs, and it has been calculated that 6 of these 8 studded pieces can be put together in nearly 1 million different combinations. Of course, that was calculated using a computer. No one actually sat down and played with Lego for a few years to find out.

Many Lego construction sets feature small vehicles with wheels, and each year, there are about 306 million of these wheels made and sold, which is more than all the real tires made everywhere. During the Christmas holiday season, there are 28 Lego sets sold every second around the world, which is over 100,000 every hour.

Anyway, let's hope that all the Lego people will never decide to take over the world- with so many around, they might even be able to do it!

There Are More Trees on Earth Than Stars In The Galaxy

Our galaxy is called the Milky Way, and it is made up of a lot of stars, including our sun. It is estimated that there are between 100 billion and 400 billion stars in the Milky Way – estimated by computer because, of course, no one could ever count them all physically; it would take far too long. An interesting fact, however, is that there really are more trees on Earth than there are stars in the galaxy.

Scientists have calculated that there are as many as 3 trillion trees globally, with most of them in the world's rainforests. Since a trillion is 1,000 billion, you can work out that even with the maximum number of stars in the galaxy, there are still 7 times more trees than stars.

Although people who care about the environment often talk about how trees are being cut down and forests being destroyed, there are actually more trees now than there were 100 years ago. Just in the past 40 years, the area of Earth covered in trees has increased from 31 million square kilometers to 35 million square kilometers.

However, since the start of human civilization, the number of trees has decreased by nearly half, especially in the centuries when people used wooden ships to travel around the world. Billions of trees were cut down to provide the wood for ships, as well as land being cleared for farming. These days, land clearance is still something that people do in places like South America, but now ships are made from steel and other materials, so not as many trees are being used for that.

Fortunately, the regions where farmers are still clearing land for crops by cutting down trees are not the most important areas for the planet. The three key areas are Canada, Siberia, and Scandinavia, where there are vast forests with temperate climates, and they are sometimes called the "lungs of the planet." What happens is that every year in June, following springtime growth, all the trees in these regions start to release fresh oxygen into the atmosphere, and this is carried by winds around the planet, so the air you breathe may have actually come from part of Russia or even Denmark.

Then, toward the end of the year, around wintertime, the process reverses, and the trees start to absorb or "breathe in" all the carbon dioxide that has built up over the year, mostly from human activities like factories and cars. This "breathing out and breathing in" is what keeps us all alive, so we must always be aware that trees are probably the most precious things on our planet.

So even though there are more trees than stars, we can never have enough, so we should always support tree-planting whenever we can – and think of trees every time we take a breath.

The Cat Piano

I am sure you will have heard dogs howling and cats meowing, but there was a time when people tried to make musical instruments using the animals' sounds with live animals. One of these was the Cat Piano. This sounds like a YouTube video of cats running around a piano keyboard, but it was quite different. It was made from a real piano with about 6 cats in front of the keyboard in small cages.

When certain notes were played on the keyboard, a small hammer would come down on one of the cat's tails, making them howl, so the piano playing was accompanied by "singing cats." The idea seems to have been invented in about 1650 to relieve the depression of a bored Italian prince.

A court musician created the cat piano to play for the prince, and as the music played on, the cats' meowing became louder, making the prince laugh and relieving his boredom.

While this sounds like a really crazy idea, it happened on a number of occasions in different ways. In the 1600s, there was a similar entertainment for royalty, this time in Germany, where six cats were in cages together with strings tied to their tails. Instead of a human player, they had a live bear that would pull the strings and make the cats howl. Of course, no one thought this was music, but it was the sort of thing that people did for fun in those days.

The idea of the cat piano was later used in the 1800s to cure mental patients. At the time, the asylum doctors thought that the music and the cats wailing would stimulate the brains of patients who would not respond to anything else. This might sound ridiculous to us nowadays, but records from that time show that it might even have worked.

On a different note, someone created a pig piano in 15th-century France for King Louis XI. It was similar to the cat piano but using pigs. The pigs were chosen for different sizes and were lined up on a board, going from small piglets up to large pigs. The keyboard behind them was attached to poles, and when notes were played on the piano keyboard, a pole would poke a pig in the rear, making it squeal. The cacophony of pigs squealing must have been a terrible noise, but it seemed to amuse the king, who had a reputation for being a little eccentric anyway.

These days, no one would get away with mistreating any animal like that, so it is unlikely you will ever get to see or hear a cat or pig piano, which is a good thing for our ears. Some people train their pet dogs to "sing" or howl along with music, and that is bad enough!

How Old is Your Body?

If anyone asked you that question, you would probably reply with your age at your last birthday, but that is not quite true because that is just how long you have been on the planet. There are different ways of looking at age, and one of them is by looking at how old are the cells that make up all the parts of your body.

Cells don't last forever, however. They wear out and can get damaged without us even noticing, and the majority of cells that make up our skin and internal organs are replaced every 7 to 10 years. The only cells that stay with us throughout our lives are our brain cells, which is important because they contain all the information about us, who we are, and what we know, so they never change except to grow more as we grow up.

Here are some examples of cells that are renewed regularly: muscles are renewed regularly as we move around and exercise and are completely replaced every 15 years. Skin cells, however, don't last that long, and you get completely new ones every 14 days. Bone cells also grow new ones every day and are all completely replaced every 10 years. So, someone who is 12 years old may have a body with parts that are almost new!

Of course, we are only talking about the parts you cannot see. The replacement and regrowth of cells can also be seen in more obvious ways, for example, your hair and nails. You can easily see them growing new cells every day, and that is exactly what happens inside your body as well.

So, you might ask, why are there old-looking people around, and why doesn't everyone look young all the time? Well, it seems we are like cell phone batteries, and our bodies are not designed to last forever. Our cells are programmed to divide and multiply, always making new ones. But over time, this process slows down, and some cells just stop making new ones.

A lot of this has to do with the environment and our daily lives because things like air pollution, the amount of exercise, and what we eat or drink can have an impact. If a cell gets too damaged, it just won't renew anymore, and you can see that if you have a scar – the skin around the scar might renew after a couple of weeks, but the cells that make up the scar are just too damaged, so they stay that way forever.

Regular exercise helps our cells to remain active and keep working for us, and people who exercise a lot always look younger because their cells keep renewing. Those of us who never exercise make our cells lazy, too, so they will do less work and make our bodies look older.

Of course, it is not quite that simple, but it has been shown scientifically that in order to keep looking young and healthy, it is important to have fresh, clean air, a good healthy diet, and plenty of exercise. Unfortunately, even for those of us who follow that sort of lifestyle, our cells will wear out eventually, but that's probably a good thing – imagine how crowded the Earth would be if everyone who was ever born was still alive!

The Magic of Fungus

The fungus isn't really magical, but it is one of the most useful things on our planet. It may one day even help us build something on Mars where people could live.

The most common type of fungus that we know is the mushroom, which grows in damp, dark, warm conditions like most varieties of fungus. It is also the mold that we see growing on stale food or on wood that is hidden from sunlight.

Fungus is everywhere, and spores are blowing around all the time. It is estimated that in the average home, there are up to 100 different types of fungus growing, especially in dark, damp areas. This is worse in modern homes with today's heating systems to make sure we never feel cold, which is great, but it encourages the growth of other organisms like fungus and mold. This is not good for people with allergies or asthma, and often, for them, it is better to just wrap up warm in a cold room rather than have a hot, humid atmosphere.

Another type of fungus growth is yeast, which is primarily used when making bread. A type of yeast mold is also found on our heads, and on the average scalp, there are around 10 million yeast cells, which scientists think stop the skin from drying out and protect it against microbes. The yeast cells live for about a month and then fall off as what we call dandruff, and new ones grow to replace them.

We can probably thank fungus for us actually being in the world today – it is believed that fungal infections killed off most of the dinosaurs and other large predators, and that allowed mammals to grow and develop without being eaten up all the time, and they eventually evolved into various species including humans.

Mold is an ingredient in most laundry detergents, and it is mold enzymes that virtually "eat" the stains on our clothes. Mold growths are also used in drinks like beer and even in sparkling drinks like fizzy lemonade or similar drinks. The mold enzymes provide that sharp, bitter-sweet taste of the drink.

NASA is currently experimenting with a type of fungus called mycelium, which is something like the underside of mushrooms, and they are trying to grow it in sheets like plywood. When it comes to the time when men will go to Mars, it would be very difficult and expensive to transport materials to build a structure for them to live in. So, scientists at NASA are thinking about just sending the equipment to grow the mycelium fungus on Mars, which would then be used to construct a building.

They are also working on a type of algae that could be combined with the fungus, an alga that reacts to sunlight like a plant and will produce oxygen, and the mycelium and the algae together will make a place where people can live. This all sounds very science-fiction, but it is happening, and one day people may live on Mars in houses made out of fungus that produce their own atmosphere.

Finally, we should all know about the fungus that saves lives every day. Penicillin is a drug that is used to fight many diseases and infections, and penicillin comes from a type of mold. So maybe fungus is magical after all?

Why Does the Earth Spin?

We are always curious creatures, and we are always wondering why things happen in a certain way. For example, why do noses run and feet smell? There is so much about the world around us that seems like a mystery, but if we look around enough, we can usually find an answer. One thing we don't think about very often in our daily life is why the Earth spins.

To understand this, we need to go back in time to when the Earth was first formed, about 5 billion years ago. Our sun was formed by the collapse of a huge cloud of particles in something like a nuclear explosion. There were a lot of bits of rock and rubble left over from the explosion, which started to spin around the sun like water going down a plughole, and all these bits gradually stuck together and formed the Earth, which kept spinning around the sun. It keeps spinning because there is nothing to stop it.

If a girl is playing with a hula hoop in her garden, she has to keep moving the hoop so it keeps spinning around her body. If she stops moving, the friction of the air and the pull of gravity will slow the hoop down, and it will stop spinning. However, out in space, there is no gravity and no air, so if something starts spinning, it just keeps going forever. Actually, that is not quite true of the Earth. The moon exerts a little bit of gravity on the Earth, causing the tidal motion of the oceans, and it also slows the Earth down a little, making a difference of 1 second every 50,000 years.

The Earth spins completely around every 24 hours and also moves around the sun, and it takes it 1 year to go around completely. The Earth cannot stop spinning, and even if another planet or asteroid hit the Earth, it would probably just spin in a different way. However, if the Earth did stop spinning, we wouldn't all just fall off; gravity would still keep us on the ground, but many other things would change. If we still went around the sun, half the year, one side would face the sun, so one day would last 6 months, and half the year, that side would face away from the sun, giving us 6 months of night.

The whole climate would change, and the change in temperature would cause strong winds as warm air moves toward cold air.

The Earth's core is molten metal, and the spinning of the Earth makes this metal magnetic, and this provides a magnetic field around the Earth, which protects us from the sun's radiation. Without the magnetic field, the radiation would cover the planet and make everyone very sick, and birds would get lost because they use the magnetic field to find their way, for example, when they fly south for winter and come back for spring.

The worst thing to happen if the Earth stopped spinning is that everything would be thrown around and destroyed. The Earth spins at about 1,100 miles per hour, and if it stopped, the atmosphere would keep spinning for a while until it stopped as well. That means something like an enormous rush of air at 1,100 miles an hour would tear everything off the ground and throw it around the planet like paper caught in a sudden wind.

Luckily, as I said, this will never happen, and as long as the Earth keeps turning, everything will be fine. It's the brightest object in the night sky and endlessly fascinating. When you look at the full moon, you might see what looks like a human face, a human head, or even a full-size human figure.

Where did the man in the moon come from?

In some legends, he was sent there as punishment for a crime he had committed, such as working on the Sabbath or holy day of the week. The image of the moon looks different in the Northern and Southern Hemispheres, and the legends are different, too. In the Northern Hemisphere, The Sea of Serenity and the Sea of Rain form the man's eyes; his mouth is made up of the Sea of Clouds; and the Sea of Vapours and the Sea of Islands make up his nose.

For the Norse, Mani the Moon is forever crossing the sky in his carriage, drawn by horses, pursued forever by Hati, the Great Wolf, who finally catches him at Ragnarok, or the destruction of the world.

In Korea and Japan, the rabbit on the moon is always pounding away at ingredients to make medicine or rice cakes. In other tales, a wolf falls madly in love with a toad. Not trusting the wolf, the toad took a huge leap - and ended up on the moon.

Old Chinese myths say it is a goddess, Chang'e, who has drunk a double helping of a potion to make herself immortal - and found herself on the moon. Yu Tu, a rabbit or hare, is there to keep her company in some versions of the tale. A Vietnamese tale tells of a Moon Lady and a Jade Rabbit on the moon - they are celebrated at a festival in Mid-Autumn.

The scientific explanation for why we see the man in the Moon (or the Lady, the Rabbit, or the Toad) lies in how we see the light and shadow on the moon's surface. The moon is locked in orbit with the same face always facing towards us - we're always looking at the same surface. For many centuries, people believed there was water on the moon - which is why many of the flat areas on the satellite are called seas or "maria." We now know that these seas are actually huge expanses of hardened lava. The volcanic rock doesn't reflect as much light as the rest of the surface of the moon. The brighter areas are the highlands.

You might be wondering why we see a Man at all (or any of the other creatures). And this is due to a condition called pareidolia, where we see shapes in clouds, on vegetables, or on the moon.

The moon isn't the only heavenly body where people think they've spotted faces. In 1976, when the Viking 1 spacecraft made it as far as Mars, many people thought the images showed a face on the surface. As our photography and technology have improved, we know it's just a trick of the light.

Can You Really Travel to the Four Corners of the Earth?

If you want to see for miles and miles, one of the best ways is to climb a hill, right? But did you know that there are some parts of the world where you can see not only your own state or county but right into other states, countries, or territories?

And one of those is the Four Corners. It gets its name from the fact it takes in the following corners: north-western New Mexico, north-eastern Arizona, south-eastern Utah, and southwestern Colorado, and there's a monument to mark the spot. Other tourist spots nearby are Chaco Canyon, Mesa Verde National Park, Monument Valley, and the Canyons of the Ancients.

Most of this region is in the ownership of the Navajo Nation, the Hopi, the Zuni, or the Ute, and this dry, rural area is part of a much larger region called the Colorado Plateau.

There's even a special name for these types of places: if you can see three different counties or countries, they're called tripoints; if the total is four, they're called quadripoints.

And the US isn't the only place in the world where you'll find them.

Legend has it that, on a clear day, you can see England, Ireland, Scotland, and Wales from the top of Snaefell, a small mountain on the Isle of Man in the UK. This part of the world is known for its generally damp and misty climate, however, so you'll need to plan carefully to manage to see this view.

And then there's Säntis, the highest peak in what's known as the Alpstein massif, located in northeast Switzerland. From here, you can see six European countries, weather permitting: Austria, France, Germany, Italy, Liechtenstein, and Switzerland.

Then there's Ljuboten, a mountain on the border between Macedonia and Kosovo in Europe. From here, you can see Albania, Bulgaria, Greece, Kosovo, Macedonia, Montenegro, and Serbia – seven countries in all.

There are over a hundred and fifty tripoints on the planet, but there's only one quadripoint that can be truly called international. It's located in southern Africa. Look for a spot where Botswana, Namibia, Zambia, and Zimbabwe meet, right in the middle of the waters of the Zambezi River.

There are plenty of tripoints, however – including France, Germany, and Switzerland; Argentina, Brazil, and Paraguay; Venezuela, Guyana, and Brazil; and Finland, Norway, and Sweden. The tripoints are often found where rivers meet, and though monuments and other markers are often used to highlight the location, they might not be exactly on the border.

Conclusion

You've just traveled through a world of wonders and arrived at the end of *Fascinating Stories for Curious Minds*. Hopefully, these stories have opened your eyes to the amazing and often times weird world around us. From the depths of space to the quirks of pop culture, we've seen that our universe is an amazing puzzle with endless pieces. These stories remind us to keep asking questions, to look closer at the world, and to find joy in the mysteries that are still unsolved. Keep these stories in mind as you go about your days, and remember that every day is a chance to find something fascinating in the world around us.

Thank you for buying our book!

If you find this storybook fun and useful, we would be very grateful if you could post a short review on Amazon! Your support does make a difference and we read every review personally.

If you would like to leave a review, just head on over to this book‘s Amazon page and click "Write a customer review."

Thank you for your support!

Printed in Great Britain
by Amazon

35331567R00121